iPHONE
Millionaire

✓

iPHONE
Millionaire

How to Create and Sell Cutting-Edge Video

MICHAEL ROSENBLUM

Founder of the New York Video School

New York   Chicago   San Francisco   Lisbon   London   Madrid   Mexico City
Milan   New Delhi   San Juan   Seoul   Singapore   Sydney   Toronto

The *McGraw-Hill* Companies

1 2 3 4 5 6 7 8 9 0   DOC/DOC   1 0 9 8 7 6 5 4 3 2

ISBN: 978-0-07-180017-4
MHID: 0-07-180017-4

e-ISBN: 978-0-07-180018-1
e-MHID: 0-07-180018-2

McGraw-Hill books are available at special quantity discounts to use as premiums and sales promotions, or for use in corporate training programs. To contact a representative, please e-mail us at bulksales@mcgraw-hill.com.

Library of Congress Cataloging-in-Publication Data

Rosenblum, Michael
      iphone millionaire : how to create and sell cutting-edge video / by Michael Rosenblum.
            p.   cm.
         ISBN-13: 978-0-07-180017-4 (alk. paper)
         ISBN-10: 0-07-180017-4 (alk. paper)
         1. Video recordings—Production and direction.   2. Video recording.   I. Title.
      PN1992.94.R68 2012
         791.43—dc23   2012017118

This book is printed on acid-free paper.

To my wife Lisa

Contents

Acknowledgments

First and foremost this book is dedicated to my lovely wife Lisa, without whose love and support none of this would have been possible. She met me at a very different point in my life, not so many years ago, when I was at the nadir of my existence. She scraped me off the floor and gave me the confidence and courage to start again. At the very beginning, when all looked hopeless she said "one day you will write a book entitled *Suicide to Success*." I didn't believe her then, but I do now and here it is. Of course, my editor at McGraw-Hill, Mary Glenn came up with a much better title, and I am deeply indebted to her for her support and belief, as well as to my agent Jennifer Griffen at The Miller Agency, who took me on when no one else would. I would also like to thank Michael Tannen, who made all of this possible a long time ago, along with the late Jan Stenbeck; Paul Sagan, Pat Younge, Mark Bittman, Carl Spielvogel, Pat Loughrey and Kevin Klose, who bought into what must have seemed some crazy ideas at the time; and "B," who is now prepared to take this to the next generation.

Introduction

 How a Wasted Childhood Led to the Opportunity of a Lifetime

I grew up in front of a TV set.

While the other kids in the neighborhood were out playing baseball or riding their bikes, I was busy watching *Leave It to Beaver* or *Gilligan's Island* or *The Addams Family*. As soon as I got home from school, I would position myself in front of the TV, my face inches from the screen, a box of Froot Loops clutched in my hands.

My days started early, with cartoons at 5 a.m. If I got up before that, there was always *The Modern Farmer* or *Agriculture USA* with its endless shots of combines, cows, and soybeans. By the time I was eight years old, I knew all about how to maximize your crop yield.

Half-hour after half-hour, day after day, year after year, the never-ending contents of TV poured directly into me. I was a child TV addict. *The Munsters*, *Green Acres*, *Petticoat Junction*, *Million Dollar Movie* (which aired not once but twice: "If you have missed any part of *Forbidden Planet* or would like to see it again, it will be shown in its entirety following station identification.") Entire weekends would be spent in front of the tube. "Monsters, John. Monsters from the id!"

My father used to yell at me that I was wasting my life in front of that "stupid TV set." "Get out of the house and do something!"

I ignored him. I was doing something. I was watching TV.

Now, my old man may have been annoyed at me, but how many of those neighborhood kids tossing around a ball became professional baseball players? How many of those kids tooling around town on their bikes ended up riding in the Tour de France?

I, on the other hand, knew that I had found my calling. I became a successful TV producer. To this day, I can still sing the missing verse from the *Gilligan's Island* theme song: "So this is the tale of our castaways, they're here for a long long time...."

Who else do you know who can tell you that Dobie Gillis went to S. Peter Pryor Junior College?

When I was ending my ten-year relationship with my French girlfriend, I explained our incompatibility by singing the *Mister Ed* song.

"A horse is a horse," I began.

She stared at me. "Oui... that is true," she said, with that adorable French accent.

"Exactly!" I said, as though I were Pierre Curie discovering radium. "Because the correct answer to 'a horse is a horse' is 'of course, of course,' and that is why we have to break up."

Little did I know that in all those thousands of wasted hours I was, in fact, preparing myself for a career. A career in the world's easiest multi-billion-dollar industry: television.

A career that today is open to anyone.

Or at least anyone with an iPhone or a video camera in their closet.

Yes, it's true. Watching TV, hour after hour, day after day, I was actually teaching myself how to make TV shows, and it turns out that making TV shows is always in great demand.

My guess is that you might have invested similar time and effort in TV watching, but perhaps without benefiting from the results—at least until now.

I am going to show you how to put all those hard-earned hours in front of the tube to work for you.

We are a TV nation. The average American spends five hours a day, every day, watching TV. This takes place 365 days a year. That's a lot of TV.

So it turns out that despite what Dad said, I was not the only one wasting my life away in front of a TV set.

We Americans spend more time watching TV than we do playing sports, eating, reading, knitting, bowling, or any one of a thousand other activities. TV watching is, in fact, our number one pastime.

We are the world leaders in TV watching—the Olympic champions.

But wait, there's more. (And if that phrase sounds familiar, you are already close to a very successful career.)

Because not only do we spend five hours a day watching TV, we spend a mind-boggling eight and a half hours a day staring at screens— TV screens, computer screens, smart phone screens, and tablet screens— not to mention billboard screens.

Eight and a half hours a day staring at screens means that we will spend more of our lives watching screens than we will spend doing anything else, including sleep. Screen watching is now our number one activity, and we're just getting started.

Most of the stuff you're going to see on those screens, from laptops to smart phones, is going to be in video—because TV no longer means what's on Channel 9 at 5 p.m. Now, TV means anything in video, and that video can be on the plasma screen on your wall, on your laptop, on your iPad, or on your phone. It's all video, and it's all TV.

Not only are you going to be seeing video on your phones, iPads, and computers, but you're also going to be seeing it on billboards, on the sides of buildings, and on the sides of buses. Where you once saw posters and billboards, you're now going to see video. A world awash in video.

Video, 24 hours a day, 7 days a week, 365 days a year. Millions and millions and millions of hours of it.

Who is going to make all that video?

It could be you.

It should be you, because making video is going to become the biggest growth business of the next decade.

That's right.

Someone is going to have to make all the stuff that is going to fill all those screens. This is a multi-trillion-dollar business that doesn't even exist yet. The opportunity of a lifetime. Who is going to seize it?

You.

And you know why?

Because you already know how to do it.

You do.

You just don't know that you know it...yet. But if you give me six weeks, I will make you into a professional video and TV producer. Because I am going to tap into what you already know—in fact, what you've already dedicated years studying.

I am going to put you on the leading edge of what is going to be the biggest boom industry since gold was discovered at Sutter's Mill in California in the 1800s.

■■■ Who, Me?

You might say, well, that's fine for you. You were a TV producer. I understand that you know how to make video and TV shows. But what about someone with no experience whatsoever?

Here's the best part: The less "professional" experience you have, the better off you are!

How come?

Two reasons: First, in the olden days (which ended yesterday), it was really expensive to get into the TV business. A broadcast-quality video camera could cost as much as a hundred thousand dollars. A professional video editing suite could run as much as a million dollars, not to mention the lighting, the audio, the studios, and the skills. People who have worked in the industry do things in a very expensive and time-consuming way.

Today, the high-definition (HD) video camera that came with your iPhone is most likely a better camera than the "professional" cameras that most TV shows have been made with. That camcorder you've been taking on your vacations? That's probably professional-level gear. The free video editing software on your laptop is more powerful than that million-dollar editing suite of yesterday.

And the second reason: All this gear has been made totally automatic. The cameras are totally automatic point-and-shoot, and the editing software is so simple that pretty much any 12-year-old can edit a movie on his or her own.

Broadcast-quality gear. Any idiot can do this.

It's a powerful combination.

Just how much demand is there going to be?

In the 1970s, when there were only three TV networks, there was a total demand for about 40,000 hours of television content per year, more or less. That was an amount that could be met by the networks and a few Hollywood studios.

By the 1990s, when there were 500 cable channels, the demand for content had skyrocketed to more than 2 million hours a year. Is 2 million hours a lot? Let's put it this way: If you live to be 85 years old, you will only live 750,000 hours. So 2 million hours of video content per year is a ton.

Then, as if that were not enough, the web went to video. This year, average people, people like you and me, will upload a mind-boggling 48 hours of video every minute. Every minute. For a total of some 20-plus billion hours of video online. Today, people view an average of 3 billion hours of video on YouTube every month. NBC, by way of comparison, broadcasts about 750 hours of video every month. Do you see where all this is headed? And we're just getting started. Add in the need to fill the screens of every iPhone, every smart phone, every tablet, and you have a pretty limitless demand for video content.

▪▪▪ How Much Money Could I Make?

Today, the average cable networks pay about $250,000 per half-hour for the shows you are watching. (Amazing, huh? And they generally buy in blocks of 13 shows.)

So, if I said to you, "Would you be up for shooting and producing a reality show in your hometown, on your iPhone, for, say, $200,000 a half-hour?" Would you go for that?

How about $150,000?

How about $100,000?

Anyone in the room willing to do it for $80,000? $75,000? Do I hear $70,000?

Anyone here willing to make the show for $60,000? $50,000?

How about $30,000? Thirty thousand dollars to shoot and cut 22 minutes' worth of content?

Hands down.

You see where this is headed?

Now, do you think the networks are interested in hearing from you? You bet they are! And are you interested in taking a crack at this? You'd be crazy not to.

It's a win/win . . . except, of course, for the folks who own those big, fancy production companies and studios in New York and Los Angeles. But hey, haven't they made enough money already?

Now it's your turn.

▪▪▪ Can I Really Do This?

If you are like me—if you are like most people—you've spent far too many hours watching TV already. Or movies. The funny thing is that you have unwittingly been educating yourself in what I would call *video literacy*. You already know what it's supposed to look like. You know what works and what doesn't.

And, if you're like most people, you watch stuff on cable and think: I could do that. Indeed, where do you think reality TV came from?

Well, the good news is that you can. You can do this. And the better news is that I am going to teach you how to do it. And the whole thing is going to take you about six weeks or less.

That's it.

Six weeks to change your life.

Six weeks to a whole new career.

Over the past 25 years, I have invented an entirely new way of creating and producing video that has nothing to do with the "traditional" methods they teach at film or journalism schools. The new technologies of small digital cameras and laptop editing software have opened the door to an entirely new approach—one that anyone can learn in, quite literally, a few hours. That is what I am going to teach you.

■ ■ ■ And Who Are You?

I have spent my life teaching people how to make video and TV on their own using simple equipment and tapping into what they already know.

I have trained more than 30,000 people in my four-day intensive boot camps, which I hold worldwide. I have produced thousands of hours of award-winning cable TV and reality shows using these simple methods.

I have designed, built, and "retreaded" TV stations and entire networks based on these ideas, from Time Warner's NY1 in Manhattan, to KRON/4 in San Francisco, to the BBC's entire national network, to the Voice of America, to Eri TV in Eritrea, and many more. My media clients include Condé Nast, McGraw-Hill, the *New York Times*, Sky Sports in the United Kingdom, German State Television, Swedish TV, Danish TV, Dutch Public TV, the Palestinian Broadcast Authority, the United Nations, and many more.

But now, if you stick with me, I am going to take you into the world of professional broadcasting and teach you to make millions.

■ ■ ■ A Final Note

The video camera on your iPhone or in your closet is good enough to create professional-quality video. All you need to know is what to do with it and how to sell it. This is what I am going to show you.

At the end of the day, you will be measured solely by what you put on the screen.

No one cares where you went to school, what kind of gear you are using, or how long you have been doing this. None of this matters. All that matters is that the final product you produce is great. This is all that people care about.

I will teach you how to do this and how to sell it. The ideas of what to put on the screen, I leave to you.

1

Your First Week:
Anyone Can Do This

In this week, we're going to get an overview of how the world of television, video, and film has changed and how you can be part of a massive new opportunity. The less experience you have, the better.

In the early 1990s, I was teaching at Columbia University's Graduate School of Journalism.

Everyone says, "Don't date your students," and this, it turns out, is very good advice. I wish I had listened. In 1992, I started to date one of my students. In 1993, I married her. And in 2003, I filed for divorce. But it's the dating part that we are interested in at the moment.

She was an aggressive 23-year-old who had worked for an English-language newspaper in Mexico City and now wanted to expand her journalism education.

I had graduated from Columbia's Graduate School of Journalism only a few years earlier and had found a job working as a producer for *CBS Sunday Morning*, the CBS News program. With this, I was qualified to get a part-time position as an adjunct professor at Columbia teaching television.

I met Glenda at the student-faculty mixer, and to move our burgeoning relationship along, I suggested that it might be fun to shoot a "documentary film" together.

And thus it was that we spent a weekend in Philadelphia in the Emergency Room of the Hospital of the University of Pennsylvania, called HUP. We had brought our video camera, a small handheld home video camera, in the hopes of shooting a real-life version of *ER*, the very popular TV show.

A great deal of "documentary filmmaking" is just a matter of showing up with a camera and waiting for something "interesting" to happen—then filming it. Emergency rooms are good places to wait for "interesting things" to happen. You sit and wait, and interesting things just come in through the door.

While we were in the ER waiting room, a young couple came in with an interesting story.

The core of any good film or video is in the characters. Casting is everything. And you don't get any good characters unless you start casting, so that is what I did. I leaned over and said to the guy who had just entered the ER, "How are you doing?"

This, in retrospect, seems a stupid question in a hospital emergency room.

The guy looked at me for a second. He was a big, menacing man with a mean expression, and I thought he might punch me in the face for having the temerity to talk to him, but then he saw the camera.

"Documentary filmmakers," I said, pointing at Glenda and myself. So he smiled.

Video cameras are licenses to be just about anywhere and talk to anyone.

"TV?" he asked. Clearly, "documentary filmmakers," while holding sway with graduate students, didn't have the traction that TV has with the general public.

I smiled. "You bet!" I said. (Who knew? Could be?)

He smiled again, clearly at ease now. TV was something he understood. It's a shared fraternity. We all do it. Five hours a day. And who does not want to be on TV?

"I was shot six times," he said, leaning in a bit and sharing a confidence.

Well, you don't see that every day.

In fact, I had never until then even met anyone who had been shot even once, let alone six times. Of course, I had seen people shot in the movies. They fell down. They died. Maybe he was pulling my leg.

"Come on," I said, ever the journalist with the incisive question.

He could see that I did not believe him. A dark scowl crossed his face, which was pretty scary.

"You wanna see?" he asked, more intimidating than questioning.

Of course I did, and he lifted his shirt to reveal six small black bumps. "Bullets," he said.

"I was shot too," his girlfriend added, somewhat competitively. "In the butt. You wanna see that?"

He shot her a glance that indicated that she was clearly not to drop her pants.

Just then, the attending nurse indicated that my new gunshot victim/friend could come into the emergency room and be seen.

"Can Mister TV man come along?" he asked the nurse. "He gonna put me on Channel 5 news."

The nurse rolled her eyes and said, "Sure."

"This gonna be on TV, right?" my new friend asked me.

"You bet!" I said. What was he going to do if it wasn't? Shoot me? Probably. Anyway, all four of us headed into the ER.

Now, as it turns out, when you get shot, particularly with a small-caliber bullet, so I am told, you don't fall down dead like on *Law and Order*. Sometimes the bullet just enters the body, and it's fast and hot, and the wound cauterizes and the bullet just stays there and ultimately works its way to the surface, like a splinter.

In the ER, a doctor on call showed me this miracle. He lifted our "victim's" shirt, and with a straightened paper clip, he tapped the top of the black bump.

Click…click…click.

"Hear that?" the doctor asked. "Metal on metal. That's the bullet."

"Cool."

The attending that day in the ER was a young woman doctor who took no liking to these kinds of people.

Frequent fliers, she called them. "Sew them up, send them out, and they get shot up again." She placed the new star of our soon-to-be documentary film on a table and began to extract the first bullet from him, without any anesthesia. She simply grabbed a set of forceps and began digging around.

My newfound friend with the six bullets screamed a scream I hope never to hear again.

The doctor put down the forceps and looked at this giant of a man, easily twice her size, and said, "You big baby."

He stopped screaming and stared at her.

For a moment.

Then she went back to work digging around.

He screamed more. Then the first bullet came out.

She held it in the forceps in front of him.

"Doesn't that feel better?" she asked.

He looked at her.

"That do *not* feel better," he said.

We were quite happily filming all of this with our video camera.

Then, with the camera rolling, the man's girlfriend reached over and grabbed the bullet from the forceps and shoved it in his face.

"You said you were shot with a .38," she said. "This ain't no .38. This is a Glock 9 millimeter."

Really.

It was a fantastic moment. And we had recorded it all.

Well, I thought, maybe this *will* be on TV.

We stayed at HUP for a few more days, shooting all kinds of interesting stuff, and then we came back to New York to edit it all together.

Now, I was the "older person" in the room. I was the person with all the TV experience. I had even won a few Emmys (okay, local Emmys at Channel 13 in New Jersey, but Emmys none the less). With all my experience, I proceeded to lay out the structure of the documentary film we were now going to make.

I saw it all very clearly in my head.

"We're going to get archival footage of the Vietnam War, and we're going to cut back and forth between Vietnam medical choppers and the ER in Philly," I announced. "The medical battlefield of Vietnam came home to the battlefield of inner-city Philadelphia," I narrated in one of those deep bass PBS "important film" voices. It was great.

Glenda looked at me like I was an idiot...or very old...or both, probably.

"I'm not doing that," she said.

The student.

"You're not?" I said.

"No way, José." Like a rebellious teenager.

"Well, what do *you* have in mind?" This was going to be good. The student filmmaker's idea.

She paused.

"I want to cut this with rock music and lots of swish pans," she said.

I stared at her.

"Are you out of your mind?" I said, playing the cool professional. "This is about life and death."

"Exactly," she responded.

We then had one of those fights that young couples have that tells them that they should find other people to marry. In the end, I threw up my hands.

"Okay, okay. Learn the hard way," I said. "Go ahead. Cut it the way you want, and you'll see. It will make a piece of typical film student crap."

So she did.

She cut it exactly the way she wanted to, this 23-year-old student with no prior experience in television or filmmaking or much of anything else.

And when I saw it, all five minutes of it, it was exactly what she said she wanted it to be.

Pounding rock music. Dum-de-dum-de-dum-de-dum....

A man screams, "Don't cut off my leg." Swish pan....

Dum-de-dum-de-dum-de-dum....

Swish pan....

"My baby's gonna die...."

Swish pan....

Dum-de-dum-de-dum-de-dum....

Swish pan....

Loud scream....

Guitar sting—doiiiiiiiiinnnnnnnnnggggggggggggg.

Clearly, a PBS documentary film this was not.

I don't know what it was, but it certainly would never have aired on *CBS Sunday Morning* with Charles Kuralt.

"What do you think?" she asked.

I didn't know what to say.

As this was going on, I had been able to secure a meeting with a brand-new cable channel, one that had just started, but so small and unknown that no one, not even I, had ever heard of it.

It was called The Learning Channel, and it was then an educational channel, based in Bethesda, Maryland. Later, it would go on to become the Discovery juggernaut TLC, but then it was totally unknown and unwatched. The new head of The Learning Channel was a man named John Ford, who had come out of WHYY, the local PBS TV station in Philadelphia, so there was a PBS connection at least.

In those days, The Learning Channel was filled with informative programs about things like *The History of the Roman Empire*. "The Romans were an industrious people...," they would begin, with lots of shots of marble statues and paintings and stuff.

I was able to get a short meeting with Mr. Ford the following week at the channel's two-room offices in Bethesda. Glenda and I would take our emergency room film to show him. Who knew? Maybe he wanted to buy a documentary film about emergency rooms.

When we arrived in Bethesda, Ford and his staff were all in a small conference room, seated around an oblong table. At the front of the room was a monitor and a VHS playback deck. We had brought along a VHS of the short, five-minute cut of our documentary film—*The Real ER*. Maybe, if they liked it enough, they would give us a few thousand dollars to finish it. Who knew?

I, for one, did not have a lot of confidence in the outcome of the meeting. If I got a chance to talk before they threw us out, I would explain that we could recut it with some archival footage of the Vietnam War and how the battlefield conditions of Southeast Asia had been brought to the battlefield of inner-city Philadelphia. Ford would like that—he was from Philly. Unless he was from the inner city of Philly, in which case he probably would find it insulting. Hmm.... This was something I would have to think about.

In any event, the lights went down, and Ford put our VHS in the deck and hit "Play," and before you knew it, the room was filled with pounding rock music. Dum-de-dum-de-dum-de-dum....

A man screams, "Don't cut off my leg." Swish pan....

Dum-de-dum-de-dum-de-dum....

Swish pan....

"My baby's gonna die...."

Swish pan....

Dum-de-dum-de-dum-de-dum....

Swish pan....

Loud scream....

Guitar sting—doiiiiiiiinnnnnnnnggggggggggg.

Ford switched on the lights again.

All around the conference table, people were sitting with their mouths agape.

Slack-jawed.

Silent.

This was very far from "The Romans were an industrious people...."

I started to talk, mostly to break the silence, but also to see if I could squeeze in my Vietnam idea before they threw us out.

But Ford beat me to it.

He turned to me (since I was the guy) and said, "I want to order 13 half-hours immediately. At $200,000 per half-hour."

"What?" I asked.

"I want to order 13 half-hours," he said.

"At $200,000 a half-hour?" I asked.

He nodded. "Can you do that?"

"Yeah. I think so."

And in that moment, effectively $2.6 million slid across the table to us.

We all shook hands, and Glenda and I walked out into the bright Bethesda sunshine. Glenda, who was wearing red converse hi-tops, had a particular lilt to her walk.

I turned to her. "Well," I said, "you certainly know what you are doing!"

She looked over at me.

"And you don't, so you stay out of my edit rooms."

And that, my friends, was that.

I went on to marry Glenda, and the five-minute "taster" we had shown to John Ford went on to become TLC's most popular TV series for years, called, *Trauma, Life in the ER*.

To this day (so far at least), *Trauma* can still be seen in reruns on any number of triple-digit cable stations. *Trauma* not only ran for ten years, but it also spun off a host of children: *Paramedics*, *Maternity Ward*, *Labor and Delivery*, *Breaking News*, *Blood, Sweat and Cheers*, and God only knows how many others. It was an endless stream of reality shows, all based on the same basic concept:

Dum-de-dum-de-dum-de-dum....

Swish pan....
Loud scream....
Guitar sting—doiiiiiiiinnnnnnnnnggggggggggg.
Now what's the lesson here?
Anyone can do this.
Trust me.
Anyone.

2

The Opportunity Before You

As I said in Chapter 1, in the late 1980s, I was a TV producer for CBS News. It was a good job. I was making about $100,000 a year, which was a pretty great salary for someone in his early thirties. I had a big job at *CBS Sunday Morning*, which was an important show on the network. I was traveling all over the world to film stories. In short, I thought I was on the top of the world.

Then, one day, they sent me to interview a guy named Jim Rogers.

Rogers lived in a massive townhouse on Riverside Drive in Manhattan. He was an investment banker, in the days before anyone had even heard of investment bankers. In fact, he was a partner of George Soros. Some people said that he was the brains behind Soros. He had made billions, in the days when a billion was still a massive number. And he was not much older than me.

I asked him, "What's the secret?"

He said there was no secret. He said that all he did was look at what was happening in the world and understand what it would mean.

I had no idea what he was talking about, so I asked him for an example.

"Remember when Chernobyl blew up?" he asked.

"The reactor? Sure," I said.

"As soon as I heard about it, I went out and bought all the potato futures I could lay my hands on."

"Potatoes?" I asked.

"Yep. I knew that the fallout would render most of Russia's potato crop unsellable. The price of potatoes was going to skyrocket."

And he was right.

I learned then that the trick to making money is to take a look at what is happening around you and understand what is going to happen as a consequence.

That is the wisdom I am going to pass on to you now: To look around you and see something so obvious that you are not going to be able to believe that you didn't see it before. Then I am going to teach you how to make money out of it.

Here's a good exercise: Take a walk through any mall or Main Street in America. Do it in your own hometown. You don't have to go far. Look at the stores. What do you see? What are they selling? Ninety percent of them are probably selling clothing or food. And why are they selling clothing and food? Because clothes and food are two things that we use every day. You generally can't go wrong selling food and clothes. Everyone needs them.

Everyone eats, generally three times a day, if not more. So food is something everyone will need at some point. As a business, food is a pretty good bet. And we all wear clothes, and we generally change them every day. So clothes are also a pretty dependable business. Food and clothes can't go wrong.

Now, as you take your tour through the mall or down Main Street, you aren't going to see a lot of bookstores. Maybe one, and maybe one hardware store. You don't need three hammers a day.

But food and clothing are dependable. Hammers and books, not so much.

Now suppose that I could tell you about something that people did even more often than they eat or change their clothing. Would that interest you?

And supposing that I were to tell you that not only could you get into that business but you also could get into it both cheaply and easily.

Would *that* interest you?

I bet it would.

There is, in fact, something that we do more often than eating or getting dressed. We do it every day. It seems that we can't live without it. And while food and clothing are as old as human beings, this new "thing" appeared only yesterday, so it's virgin territory.

Remember when I told you that the average American spends five hours a day watching TV? Every day. Seven days a week. Fifty-two weeks a year.

We consume a whole lot more TV than we do McDonald's hamburgers. A whole lot more. And we spend a whole lot more on our TV than we do on McDonald's. Or Burger King. Or KFC.

Now those aren't bad businesses. It would be nice to own a McDonald's franchise. The last time I looked, a McDonald's franchise cost anywhere from $172,000 to $1.9 million. That's a big investment up front.

But you already have a franchise that can generate as much as a McDonald's franchise in your pocket right now. And it won't cost you a dime.

Got a smart phone with a video camera or a digital camera in your closet?

That's pretty much all it takes.

You have all the tools you need to start creating and selling video content.

And where is it going to go?

Take a look at your iPhone. Not only does it have a camera, but it also has a screen. It's not really a phone—it's a computer.

Got an iPad or a tablet?

Know what these things all have in common?

They all have screens.

Just like your TV.

As we begin to get more and more screens in front of us—computer screens, iPads, smart phones, and so on—we are spending even more time in front of screens.

As I mentioned when we started, the average American will spend a mind-boggling eight and a half hours a day staring at screens—TV sets, computers, phones, and tablets.

This means that screen watching is now the number one activity for all Americans. And we're just at the beginning. You will, in fact, spend more time this year staring at a screen than you will spend eating, getting dressed, playing sports, working, driving your car, or even sleeping.

More time watching a screen than sleeping.

Screen watching is now our number one activity.

It's an activity that didn't even exist one hundred years ago.

Isn't that weird?

We've all collectively decided to commit the vast majority of our lives to something that didn't even exist a hundred years ago—watching screens.

It's a whole new business opportunity.

Now, I am not suggesting selling those screens. That's a one-time event. One plasma screen or laptop or smart phone lasts you a pretty long time—and you've already got a lot of competition in that field—just ask the folks at Sony.

What I am suggesting is that you get into the business of creating and selling what is on the screens.

Online video? You can't eat it. You can't wear it. You can't live in it. But, boy, it seems to be something that no one can live without. In a recent Nielsen survey, a good percentage of Americans said that they would give up food before they gave up their Internet connections. That is something to think about!

The screens are going to need a whole lot of stuff on them. A whole lot of stuff. They have to hold our attention—and we can get bored pretty quickly.

And what is going to be on those screens?

Well, it's a pretty good bet that a lot of that stuff is going to be video.

How do I know?

Today, video dominates your TV screen. But in the earliest days of cable, there were a few attempts to put text on the TV screens. There were so many new cable channels, and most of them were empty, so some pretty smart folks thought, Why not?

It was called *teletext*, and it was a big failure.

It turned out no one wanted to read the news or sports on their TV sets. They wanted to watch it.

And now, as video comes to the web and smart phones and tablets, you can be pretty sure that the vast majority of what you are going to see on those screens is also going to be video.

There is a kind of Gresham's law for media—that is, more powerful, more dynamic media tend to drive out less dynamic media. This is true in almost everything.

If you come across a printed ad for selling a car, it might look like this:

Boring!

Now, if you're selling a car, you'd do better with a photo:

4-Wheel Beauty

Save ✉ | **f Like**   **🐦 Tweet**

| Consumer Reviews | Features & Specs | Safety | Reliability |

Used from **$12,000**

CONTACT OWNER

Photos

Consumer reviews: ★★★½☆

But what happens when you start to get video? The video makes the photo ad look as weak and boring as the classified print ad. That's just human nature. More dynamic media drive out less dynamic media. So, as every newspaper or magazine or used-car dealer moves to the web, they are going to have to present their content in more and more video.

There is going to be a massive demand for video.

How much demand is there going to be?

When I graduated from college in the late 1970s, there weren't that many places you could go if you wanted to work in video. There were basically three major networks—NBC, CBS, and ABC—a few local stations, and PBS. And that was it.

Making television and broadcasting television were so complicated and so expensive that only giant media companies could afford to do it.

In those days, the big three networks shared an audience of about 100 million households every night. This meant that pretty much regardless of what they put on the air, the networks could each deliver about 30 million homes to their advertisers. And advertisers would pay a lot to get their messages in front of 30 million homes.

100 million households

3 networks

1973　　　　　　1993　　　　　　2003　　　　　　2013

If you owned a network, it was a great business, pretty much a license to print money.

On average, in those days, a good rule of thumb was that each hour of TV cost about $1 million to make. And the networks had tons of money, so spending on crews and directors and travel was no big deal. It was, in fact, a given.

When I first started working for *CBS Sunday Morning* at CBS News, I was assigned to do a piece on the Bolshoi Ballet. The Soviet ballet company was coming to the United States, and during the Cold War, this was a big deal.

The Bolshoi had a schedule that took the company to New York, Washington, DC, Miami, Houston, and Los Angeles. I asked the executive producer of the show which city I should shoot the story in. She looked at me like I was an idiot.

"All of them," she said.

And so I spent weeks following the Bolshoi all over the country.

Then, in the 1990s, a new technology came along that changed the business forever.

Cable.

Suddenly, the world went from three networks a night dividing up an audience of 100 million households to 500 or more channels dividing up the same 100 million households.

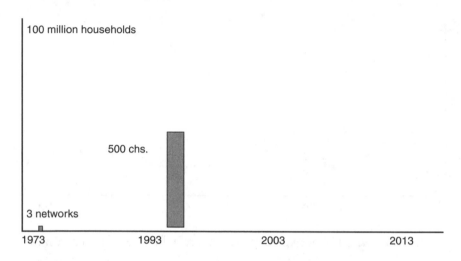

In the "olden days" of TV, if your show didn't get more than a 15 rating—that is, if you couldn't attract more than 15 percent of the households watching TV—your show was canceled. When cable came along, with its 500 channels sharing the same 100 million households, the breakeven point for TV shows began to slip. Now, instead of expecting to get 15 or even 30 percent of an audience in any given hour, a 1.0 rating was considered pretty good. That would be 1 percent of all the people watching TV in any given time slot.

A 1.0 rating meant 1 million households, more or less. And advertisers were still happy to pay to have their ads in front of 1 million households. But they weren't going to pay as much as they did when it was 30 million households.

But even a 1.0 rating would prove elusive. With 500 channels dividing the national audience each night, getting 1 percent of them would not be easy. Soon a 0.1 rating would become closer to average for most cable channels.

Well, if advertisers would pay $3 million to put a 30-second spot in front of 30 million households, how much would they pay to put a 30-second spot in front of 100,000 households (which is what a 0.1 rating translates to). The answer is not a lot.

So, by the late 1990s, the cable companies and the networks were in a jam. There were suddenly hundreds and hundreds of cable channels, all demanding content. After all, what is the point in owning a cable channel if you don't put something on it? But, while the demand for content was going through the roof, the amount of income the channels were getting was diminishing. More need for video, less money to pay for it.

Did you ever flip through your 500 cable channels and think, "There is nothing to watch here"? And now you know why.

In 1973, when there were only three networks, the total broadcast capacity of those three networks was about 64,000 hours a year. Take away the reruns and the infomercials, and you're probably at around 40,000 hours a year. This was an amount of content that the networks could reasonably handle. When the 500-channel cable environment came along, the total broadcast capacity shot up to 4.5 million hours of programming a year.

4.5 million hours!

To put this number into some kind of perspective, your entire life is about 760,000 hours long. So 4.5 million hours of programming a year, every year, is an astronomical number.

Where was all this content going to come from when there was less money to spend on it?

First, independent television production companies began to arise. They made the shows you see on cable.

Another solution that arrived around the turn of the century was reality TV shows.

In a flash, the networks got rid of the writers, the actors, and most of the production values. They used "real people" who were more than happy to appear on TV for no pay. And, as reality TV began to chow through ideas, pretty soon anything became a valid concept for a program: cupcake bakers, hoarders, tattoo parlors, annoying children. You name it...it had a show—or a series of shows.

By the same token, there are only so many truly talented people in the world, but with cable's voracious appetite for content all the time, pretty much anyone, even a "real housewife," suddenly became a star, if only for a moment. *Reality TV star* became a part of the lexicon, even if it was an oxymoron.

And, as cable began to consume more and more content, there were more and more shows for the nation to watch, so ratings continued to drop, so did revenue, and so did the amount that the cable channels could afford to pay for the programming.

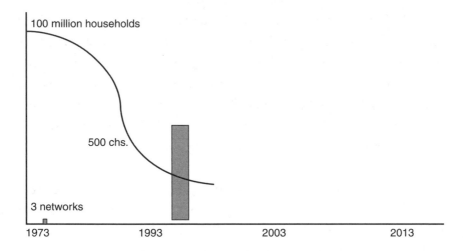

It was a kind of death spiral from which no one could escape. You have to make more programming but at lower costs. And every week there was a new cable channel or ten new cable channels, and each one demanded more programming and all at lower and lower prices because, pretty soon, 500 channels became 1,000 channels, which became 2,000 or more.

In the 1970s, the average budget for an hour of TV (which is really 44 minutes) was about $1 million. By the 1990s, when I began to produce reality TV shows, the average that the cable channels were paying for those shows was about $350,000 per hour. Today, it's closer to $150,000 an hour—and the numbers keep dropping. They have to. The audiences keep getting smaller and smaller.

And, as if that weren't enough, along came the Internet. In the beginning, it only destroyed newspapers, and the TV networks watched from a distance. But with the arrival of faster and faster connections and computers, by 2008 or so, the web began to carry video as well as cable. You couldn't tell the difference. So now, 2,000 channels threatened to become something like 2 million channels.

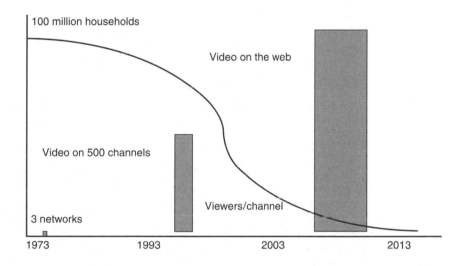

Consider this: If you think the 4.5 million hours of content on the 500 channels on cable is a lot, YouTube now has 56 billion videos, more than 30 billion hours of content, and that's just getting started.

On top of that, every smart phone, every iPad, and every website is going to consume video. There's a reason it's called "feeding the beast."

Demand for video content literally has shot through the roof, and we're only just at the very beginning of "ScreenWorld."

More channels, more platforms, more need for video, and the viewing audience growing smaller and smaller with every new channel added.

It's a funny situation: You need tons more video, and you have lots less money to pay for each individual video. There's a real problem here for networks, but there's a real opportunity here for you.

Do you see where I am going with this?

Do you think that if I could show you how to produce a really killer show with your iPhone and it looked as good as "real" TV, that the networks would be interested in talking to you?

You can count on it.

In the next few years, we're going to see a convergence of cable, broadcasting, and the web. You're going to be watching both your cable service and the Internet on your TV set, and you won't be able to tell the difference. In fact, you won't care.

ABC, NBC, Discovery Channel, YouTube, or Nike.com—what's the difference? It's all the same thing. It's all on a screen in your living room—or on your phone, for that matter.

What this means for you is that as a viewer you're going to have a lot more options. And a lot more options for you the viewer also means a lot more clients for you the low-cost producer. What this means for the networks is that where there were once 3 channels, and then there were 500 channels, soon there are going to be 10,000 channels. A hundred thousand channels. Maybe more. And all of them are going to need video. Lots of video. And at even lower cost.

And where are they going to get all that video?

If you're smart and paying attention here, you'll already know they're going to get it from you.

You are ready to start your new career.

But this part is very important: If you want to do this, I am going to ask two things of you:

First, if you have had any prior experience in the world of television, film, or video, I need you to forget everything you know or think you know.

It is not that what you have learned or done in the past is wrong, but most likely it is based on an old way of shooting and producing.

What I am going to teach you is a very simple, very efficient, and very easy way of working. But it is a way of working that is based on entirely new technologies.

So, from here on in, the only thing you know about video or TV is what I tell you. If I don't tell it to you, it doesn't exist.

If you've bought this book, you're most likely an aggressive person. You're the kind of person who always wanted to get ahead of the class. Don't do that here. Just do exactly what I tell you to do, and you will do fine. The more you adhere to exactly what I tell you, the better you will do. The more you deviate from the rules I lay down, the more difficult a time you're going to have.

A few years ago I was in London, and I got a call from Lord David Putnam. Putnam was not only a member of the House of Lords, but he was also the man who produced some of the finest motion pictures of our age: *The Killing Fields*, *Chariots of Fire*, and *The Mission*. Putnam also had run Columbia Pictures.

Putnam said to me, "I understand you have an interesting way to make films. I would like you to come here and teach it to me."

Well, it's not every day that you get a call from someone like Lord Putnam, so, of course, I agreed.

When I got to his offices in Westminster, I was incredibly nervous. First, I am in the House of Lords. Second, I am about to not just meet but also in theory "teach" one of the greatest movie producers of our time.

Putnam invited me to take a seat and said, "Okay. Teach me."

I paused for a moment, and then I just closed my eyes and thought, "What the hell."

"I need you to forget everything you know or think you know about filmmaking. From now on, the only thing you know is what I tell you. If I didn't tell it to you, it doesn't exist."

He stared at me for a long time. I am sure he was thinking, "Who is this arrogant jerk?" He listened to what I told him. Then he picked up a camera, and the two of us went out, and he started shooting.

He proceeded to ignore everything I had told him and waved the camera around wildly. Then we came back to his office to screen what he had shot.

To his credit, as we looked at what he'd shot, he beat me to the punch. "It's crap," he said.

I agreed. "Terrible."

"Okay," he said, "let's go back and do it your way." And we did. And it was...perfect.

If it works for David Putnam, it will work for you.

And the second thing:

Perfection.

I want every shot that you take to be perfect.

Here's the deal: You are in control. You will decide when to push the "Record" button. If you shoot something that is less than perfect, then you have two choices—either you put the less-than-perfect video in your final film and mess up the film. Or, if you don't use the less-than-perfect video in your final film, then all the time and effort you spent to shoot the less-than-perfect video was a waste of time. So don't do it!

You are going to live and die based on what is on the screen. No one cares how the video was made, where you went to school, how many courses you took, or how hard it was to get the video. They just don't care. And if your work is not perfect, they won't come back. You only get one chance with each viewing, so make it count.

From now on, everything you do, every shot you take, will be perfect, or you won't bother to push the button.

3

The Second Week:
Ted Turner and Me

This week you're going to learn everything you need to know about how to shoot perfect video every time.

In 1992, I wrote a letter to Ted Turner. I didn't know him and he didn't know me, but I wrote to him anyway. It was a short letter, only three paragraphs, and I got right to the point.

"You make television all wrong," I wrote. "I know a better way to do this faster and cheaper."

Then I added, "You give me ten minutes, and I will give you the world—or whatever part of it you don't own already."

Three days later my phone rang.

Ted Turner.

"You want your ten minutes? You got 'em. You be in my office at 9 o'clock tomorrow morning." And he hung up.

The next morning I was in his office at 9 a.m.

Turner barely looked at me. Instead, he glanced at his watch and said, "Go."

"You make television all wrong," I said. "You do it in a crazy and expensive way. Every one of your reporters should carry a small video camera and shoot all his or her own stuff."

"You're right," he said. "I know."

"There's a whole revolution going on with small digital cameras. Every reporter should carry one," I continued.

"You're right," he said. "I know."

"Everyone who works for the *New York Times* has a computer and knows how to write a story, even if they don't do it every day. Everyone who works for CNN should have a camera and know how to make a story. You should have hundreds of cameras in play every day... thousands."

"You're right," he said. "I know."

"I know how to cut your staffing and increase your coverage of the world all at the same time," I said.

"Stop!" he said.

Then he turned to his assistant. "Get me Pat Mitchell on the phone."

Pat Mitchell ran CNN in Atlanta.

The assistant came back. "She says she's in a meeting."

He started screaming. "You tell her she works for me, God damn it...."

In a moment, Pat Mitchell was on the speakerphone.

"Yes?"

"I got this Michael Rosenblum here in my office," Turner bellowed into the phone.

"He has this idea on how to make TV news with those little home video cameras."

He hung up the phone and turned to me.

"You get on a plane now, and you go down to Atlanta and see Pat Mitchell."

Then he came over to me. He's a big guy. I stand 5 foot, 6 inches...
on a good day.

He smacked me on the shoulder. Hard.

Pow!

"You're a smart Jew," he said.

Another smack.

"You're gonna make me a pile of money."

I like Ted Turner, and I tell you this story about him because when
he started to make his billions, he found himself in exactly the same
position that you are in right now. The only difference is that he knew it
and you didn't—until now.

Ted Turner became one of the wealthiest men in the world. He is
the largest private landholder in the United States. A few years ago he
gave a gift of $1 billion to the United Nations. Now that is rich.

But he wasn't always so rich. He made his fortune himself. And
he did it by seizing a unique moment in history—a moment just like
the one we are experiencing now.

Turner's media empire began in 1963, when he took over his father's
outdoor billboard company at the age of 24, following his father's
suicide.

The company, Turner Outdoor Advertising, was then worth $1 mil-
lion and in serious financial trouble.

Early on, Turner purchased an Atlanta UHF TV station, Channel 17.

For those of you not old enough to know the difference between
a VHF channel and a UHF channel or even have the vaguest idea of
what I am talking about, let's pause for a bit of explanation.

In the "olden days," TV did not come through cable, let alone the
Internet, which, strange to say, did not even exist. It came into your
house through the air. Maybe you have seen pictures of those old anten-
nas on the tops of people's houses. Maybe you remember having one as
a child. In any event, there were two spectrums for the transmission of
TV signals through the air. The first was VHF, which stood for "very

high frequency," and those were channels such as NBC, CBS, or ABC, the big ones that everyone watched. Then there was UHF, or "ultra high frequency," which were the channels that no one watched. Owning a UHF TV station was like owning a website that only worked on HP tablets on alternate Tuesdays.

In other words, it was the equivalent of owning next to nothing.

But Turner could see what no one else could see at the time—there was a revolution going on in the media world that was going to be a basic game changer.

Now, inventions come along all the time that change the world. And these new inventions represent huge opportunities that people seize not only to change the world but also to make fortunes for themselves. Nothing beats latching onto a new invention for a quick ride to the top. Just ask Bill Gates.

Of course, you don't even have to be the inventor. Henry Ford invented the cheap car, and everyone took to the road. Good for Henry Ford. But a lot of other folks suddenly understood the enormous opportunity that all those cars and highways meant for new businesses.

Ray Kroc saw what cars and highways meant, so he started the McDonald's chain so that all those drivers would have a place to stop and eat. Kemmons Wilson saw that all those drivers were going to need a dependable place to stay, and the next thing you know, he launched Holiday Inn. Bill Levitt, a returning World War II veteran, saw how the cars created mobility and resulted in the creation of new highways, and before you know it, he started building Levittowns all over America.

All of them saw the impact of Ford's revolution and could see just enough into the future to stake a place in the new world that was coming.

What made Turner's insight so incredibly powerful was that he saw that two new world-changing inventions could be combined to create an entirely new industry and in the process make himself billions.

The first invention was cable TV.

When cable TV was first invented, it was called CATV, for "Community Access TV," and it was a simple invention to help small towns that were prevented from receiving standard broadcast TV signals. A town might be behind a mountain that would block the broadcast signal, so the town would put a receiving antenna on top of the mountain to get the signal and then run it into everyone's house via coaxial cable. Everyone got TV by cable. Presto! Cable TV. No big deal.

Well, as it turned out, those cables could carry a lot more than the tiny handful of channels that were available over the air. Pushing a TV signal through the air required a lot of bandwidth. Running it through a wire cable allowed a lot more space for other channels. The only problem was, there were no other channels. There was a lot of excess capacity. And that excess capacity was an opportunity.

In those days, there was no Discovery Network, no National Geographic Channel, no Food Network. Nothing, in fact. So those channels sat pretty much empty.

The second invention was satellites.

After the Soviets beat the Americans into space with the *Sputnik* satellite in the 1950s, the United States spent a lot of money on putting up its own satellites. Most of those satellites, at least the ones not used for spying, were used for communications—but they were expensive.

In 1974, Western Union and NASA launched *Westar 1*, the country's first geostationary communications satellite. The satellite was supposed to be used by Western Union and the U.S. Post Office for important telegrams. NASA would go on to launch four more *Westar* satellites, some with as many as 24 transponders. That was a lot of transponder capacity for telegrams. Like the cable system, the satellite communications system in the 1970s had lots of spare capacity.

New inventions open lots of opportunities, but when you get two new inventions, particularly inventions that create spare capacity—and when you can get those new inventions to work together—well, then you've got a billion-dollar idea. And that is just what Ted Turner had.

Turner didn't have much to play with. All he had was a crummy local UHF TV station in Atlanta. There were so few people watching Turner's Channel 17 that it would have been cheaper just to stand on Peachtree Street and hand out VHS tapes with commercials on them and pay people $100 each to watch them.

With no viewers, Turner couldn't charge much for his commercials. And without much ad revenue from the commercials, he couldn't afford to buy or produce decent programming. It was an endless circle— a dead-end situation. Without better shows, he couldn't get more viewers, not that many viewers were going to tune into a UHF channel anyway. And without the money to buy those better shows, and with such a bad position on the dial, he was dead.

But Turner could see, way ahead of anyone else, that he could marry up those two new inventions—cable and satellites—to change the game, and he could be the first person to do it.

So Turner got himself a transponder on a *Westar* satellite that had a footprint over most of the United States.

Then he uplinked his fifth-rate local TV station, Channel 17, to the satellite and started beaming it down all across America.

He gave satellite dishes that could receive his signal to the burgeoning cable operators all across America so that they could get his content and put it on their empty cable networks. Now they had something else to offer their viewers.

And in an instant, Channel 17 Atlanta became Turner Superstation and then TBS, the Turner Broadcasting System.

And in that same instant, Channel 17 Atlanta went from being watched by about 25 people to being watched by about 25 million people. And that was something advertisers would pay for.

Brilliant!

And the start of a global media empire.

What Turner saw was the way to solve a problem. Here was cable, which suddenly added hundreds of new channels. What was going to go on those channels? How were you going to fill them up? For this, Turner saw another new technology—satellites. And he put the two together.

Today, we are in exactly the same position that Ted Turner was in the 1970s, except that you get to be Ted Turner this time.

Video producing is about to become the biggest growth industry the world has ever seen, and you can be part of it.

Turner had Channel 17 and satellites.

What have you got?

Got an iPhone?

Take it out of your pocket, and put it on the table.

Did you know that your iPhone has a more powerful video camera in it than professional TV has been using for most of its existence?

It's true.

That camera is HD (high definition). The first HD cameras were the size of Volkswagens and cost $1 million. How things change. Now you can own an HD video camera that costs a few dollars, and you can put it in your pocket. Oh, and it has a phone attached to it. And quite a few other things.

And for a few dollars more, you can buy a piece of video editing software that is more powerful than a million-dollar professional editing suite from the 1990s.

Amazing, huh?

Of course, you don't have to use the video camera on your iPhone. A few hundred bucks will buy you a pretty good HD video camera that is also broadcast quality. That thing you have been using to shoot all those vacation videos that no one ever looks at? It's a broadcast-quality HD camera, pal. You've got a Hollywood studio in your closet. Go get it out!

What this all means is that you already own enough equipment to shoot, edit, and produce your own cable TV show, documentary, or feature film.

Pretty cool!

I bet you didn't even realize that.

And, with a little bit of instruction, you can learn how to make your own reality show, documentary, drama, soap opera, sitcom, or anything else you want and sell it to the thousands of cable or online channels that need or are soon going to need content.

And that is what I am going to show you how to do.

■ ■ ■ Getting Started: Equipment

The first question anyone asks when starting in the world of video is, "What kind of equipment will I need?"

Even though everyone asks this question, it is the least important thing to think about when getting into the world of television and video production. It's a bit like asking, "If I want to be a novelist, what is the best kind of pencil I could get?" The correct answer is, "It doesn't really matter. It's all about the content."

However...

When asked about the cost of a yacht, J. P. Morgan once famously replied, "If you have to ask how much it costs, you can't afford it."

The same might once have been said about the video and television production business. The cameras and editing suites were so expensive that only giant corporations could afford them.

Broadcast-quality video cameras—the kind you see the camera person from your local TV station walking around with—those great, massive things on their shoulders, cost nearly $100,000.

They also weighed a ton. And they had lots and lots of very confusing buttons.

Now look at your iPhone.

Your phone has a better video camera in it than the so-called professional video cameras that TV networks have used for years. And it's a whole lot simpler to operate. It pretty much has one button—"On."

This shouldn't come as any surprise. Your phone has more computing power than the entire Apollo moon program, and it cost a whole lot less. The world of video has moved just as fast.

And it's simple! When you learn to drive a car, you don't need to know how an internal combustion engine works to get you from New York to Los Angeles. All you need to know is how to turn the key and drive.

Now, maybe you don't have an iPhone, but maybe you have a home video camera somewhere in your closet. You take it on trips from time to time, or you break it out for the kids' birthdays.

Odds are that that camera is HD. Almost every video camera produced today is.

That video camera that you have been shooting the kids' birthday parties and those trips to Disneyworld with is also vastly more powerful than all those giant "professional" video cameras that the networks used for years. In other words, you probably already have all you need to get started producing professional video right there in your pocket or in the hall closet. Isn't that surprising?

The video camera on your iPhone is 720 HD. What does that mean?

First, the 720 part.

That means that your camera is scanning 720 lines of resolution per frame.

And what in heck does *that* mean?

If you're old enough to still be buying books printed on paper, then you're old enough to remember when TV sets were those big, giant things instead of flat-screen monitors. They were built around something called a *cathode-ray tube*, which was essentially a giant vacuum tube, kind of like a giant light bulb, with a screen at the end of it.

The TV set created a picture by having an electron gun at the back of the tube (the narrow end) shoot a stream of electrons onto the front of the tube (the wide end), and by manipulating that stream electronically, the stream went back and forth, back and forth across the screen, "painting" a picture. It took 525 lines for the stream to finish one picture, from top to bottom. Then it went back to the top and started again. That was called *one frame*.

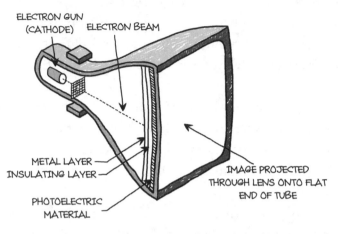

USING A CATHODE RAY TUBE AS A TELEVISION CAMERA

In America, the television standard for broadcast was called *NTSC* (after the National Television System Committee), and that standard was 525 lines to a frame and 30 frames per second. So the image that the electron gun "painted" with its 525 lines was refreshed 30 times a second. And that is why it seemed to move.

Until very recently, this was considered professional broadcast TV.

Now, the video camera on your iPhone gets a resolution of 720 lines per frame at 30 frames per second. Or to put it another way, that little video camera on your iPhone is more powerful than those massive $100,000 video cameras that professional broadcast networks have been dragging around for years.

Isn't that astonishing?

Now, as I said, the iPhone camera is as good a place to start as any, but you don't have to be limited to that. There has been a virtual explosion of HD video cameras for sale in the past few years, and all for pretty reasonable prices.

There are lots of cameras to choose from, and frankly, they're all pretty good. Like cars, with cameras you get what you pay for, but so long as the camera is HD and you can connect it to a laptop for editing (which you can pretty much do with all of them), you are ready to go.

A few years ago, traditional still camera companies such as Nikon and Canon began to manufacture 35-mm still cameras that could capture video as well as stills. These are called DSLR cameras, for "digital single-lens reflex cameras"—meaning that you see the image through the same lens that you are photographing with, through the miracle of a mirror.

DSLRs are also pretty good. What makes them interesting to people is that you can get some pretty powerful lenses on them. What makes them a bit problematic is that the video and the lenses are much better than their audio, at least as of now.

The bottom line when it comes to video is that today pretty much any video camera will do—at least to get started. As you progress in making video, you will inevitably become more familiar with the different features that different cameras bring, and you may want to upgrade or focus on one thing or another. But this will come with time and experience.

For our purposes here, pretty much any camera will do.

The same holds true when it comes to editing.

You will find lots of different kinds of editing software, from Final Cut Pro, to Avid, to Vegas Video and lots more. The good news is that they are all fundamentally the same. It's like asking what kind of car you should drive. This is a matter of personal taste, but as with cars, once you can drive one, you can drive them all.

The important thing to know about any editing software is how incredibly powerful, inexpensive, and simple to use the various types have all become. Only a few years ago, a professional video editing suite could cost as much as $500,000 and require a highly trained technician to operate.

Today, for a few hundred dollars or less, you can equip yourself with all the capabilities not just to edit but also to add graphics and effects and do a whole lot more. If you're working on a Mac, your choice is between iMovie, which comes free with your computer, and Final Cut

Pro, which costs a few hundred dollars. If you're working on a PC, your options are a bit more varied, but the principle remains the same. Once you can use one, you can use them all.

A note on audio.

It is particularly important to pay attention to audio. People will tolerate bad video (not that I am recommending that), but bad audio will alienate people immediately. When you start shooting, you really want to pay attention to the audio.

Your video camera will come with a built-in mic. Most of them are not very good. You can buy better microphones really cheaply from $40 to a few hundred. Once again, this is entirely up to you. If you're using an iPhone (or a DSLR camera), you're going to have to live with the microphone that came with the gear. In this case, it's really important to pay attention to where the microphone is when you're shooting (close to the source!), and you need to make sure that the background noise is minimized.

Lights! For the most part, you don't need them, and you don't want them.

When I was a kid, my father used to shoot 8-mm film of our birthday parties. He had massive, blinding lights on top of the camera. That was then. Today, home video cameras are so good that you can shoot your kid's birthday party with the lights from the candles. External lighting is complicated, expensive, and almost always unnecessary. If it's light enough for you to see what is going on, so can your camera. Don't worry about it.

Tripods. Like the lights, you don't want one and you don't need one. I have been shooting video for 15 years, and I have probably used a tripod about a dozen times. They are good if you are going to shoot artwork on the wall, architectural videos, or long sit-down interviews (not that anyone wants to look at long sit-down interviews). Anyone can hold a small video camera still for the ten seconds that each shot requires. Tripods are just another piece of junk that you're going to have to carry around with you that you're hardly ever going to use. My rule of thumb is the lighter, simpler, and cheaper, the better. If you must buy a tripod, get a carbon fiber one, but you won't use it much.

We are just at the very beginning of your producing career. This is going to be a career that will last you a lifetime. Ten years from now you will look back on the videos you made during these six weeks and cringe. You'll cringe because after ten years, the stuff you'll be producing will be so much better than what you'll make at the start. But we all must start somewhere.

The reason I am telling you this is to say, "Don't get hung up on the equipment." At this point, it is far less important than the content that you will produce. Slowly, over time, you'll come to understand what you need and what you don't need and what differentiates one kind of camera from another. For now, all I ask is that you have a camera or an iPhone that can shoot video and can be downloaded to editing software easily. The rest is immaterial.

4

You Already Know
How to Do This

Okay, now you have all your equipment and you're ready to begin your new life and your new career.

Nervous?

Don't be.

You're probably feeling a bit intimidated.

Maybe you're saying to yourself, "I can't do this. I didn't go to film school. I didn't go to journalism school. I don't have any experience in this. I don't know anything about film or TV or video."

Wrong!

If you're like most Americans, then you have been spending five hours a day, every day, watching TV. That's the national average.

And you didn't just start doing that yesterday. You have spent the past 20 years or so committing five hours a day, every day, to watching TV (and give yourself a few hundred hours of movies on top of that).

If you had spent five hours a day, every day, for the past 20 years practicing the piano—five whole hours a day, every day, every week, every month for even 10 years—you would be pretty good on the piano.

Well, you didn't do that.

If you had decided, at the age of five, to start spending five hours a day, every day, for the next 20 years practicing tennis—no matter what, rain or shine, you were out on the court whacking the ball around— then by now you would be a pretty good tennis player. In fact, you'd probably be nationally seeded, right?

But you didn't spend five hours a day, every day, week after week, month after month, year after year practicing your tennis game, did you? And you didn't spend it practicing the piano, did you?

Nope?

Just how did you spend all those 36,400 hours? (Astonishing, isn't it?)

You spent them watching TV or going to the movies.

Well, congratulations.

You are a world-class expert on what TV shows and movies are supposed to look like.

No,...seriously.

According to Malcolm Gladwell, author of the best-selling book, *Outliers*, 10,000 hours spent at anything can make you an expert.

And look at you! You have spent three times that gaining expertise in something much better than tennis or piano playing. You are already an expert on the most popular and lucrative activity in the world today—video-driven information and entertainment.

The problem is that until now at least, you didn't know that you were already an expert. All that's missing is how to put that expertise into practice. This is what I am going to show you. I am going to show you how to unlock the treasure-house of knowledge you have already acquired. As you will soon see, though, this isn't all that hard to do. In fact, it's simple.

Remember how your mother said that you were wasting your time watching all that TV?

Well, she was wrong. You weren't. You were, in fact, busy educating yourself as to what film and video are supposed to look like.

Now maybe you've shot a few times with a video camera on vacation or something. Maybe you've never touched a video camera at all! Better,...in fact, great!

For the past 25 years, I have been running video training boot camps all over the world teaching people to make TV on their own. I have taught thousands of people to do this. And I always start the boot camps by saying the same thing:

"If you have any prior experience in this business, if you went to film school, if you worked in TV or video, I need you to forget everything you know or think you know because all of it is wrong. From now on, the only thing you know is what I tell you. If I don't tell it to you, it doesn't exist."

See how simple this is?

In my experience, the people who do the best in this are the ones who have no prior experience at all. The rest are a bit infected, but I can unwind their bad habits as well.

I know that you can become a very successful television and video producer based on what you already know from watching TV and the movies. How do I know? Because that is exactly how I became a very successful television and video producer.

When I graduated from college, I didn't start looking for a job in TV. In fact, working in TV was the furthest thing from my mind.

I was a graduate student in Islamic history at New York University. Can you get more geeky than that? My days were spent reading Koranic texts and trying to make heads or tails of the rule of the Caliphs Omar and Uthman.

Like all graduate students, though, I needed money. Then, one day I read an ad in the *New York Times* from a company called Career Blazers. The ad said that the company was looking for "college graduates" and promised "creative careers." What the company actually was looking for was temps, and the jobs were very creative, if you think putting a stack of documents into alphabetical order is creative.

Since I had taken a typing course in high school—perhaps the best thing I learned in high school—I was eligible for one of the company's higher-paying jobs—typing. In those days, I could type 60 words per minute with no mistakes. (That was manual typewriters for you.) The job paid about $5 an hour, which was pretty good money in those days. The company used to call me in the morning and give me my assignment. I would get sent to a bank, an insurance company, or a law firm and spend my days typing transcripts from recordings of depositions or dictated letters. Then one day, the company sent me to a TV studio.

Now, like anyone else, I had watched lots of TV, but the idea of working in TV had never really occurred to me. And this was a TV newsroom at that. In fact, this was a network TV newsroom. It was the offices of *Good Morning America*, ABC's morning news show.

My job, like all the other temp jobs I had had before, was to sit at a desk all day long and type transcripts. Not very demanding. Put on a set of headphones, and type out transcripts of what had been on the show. Well, typing transcripts of the shows was at least a bit more interesting than typing out legal depositions all day.

I had been on the job for about three days when suddenly, one morning, all hell broke loose. Phones were ringing, people were running around screaming, papers were flying. It was utter chaos.

Of course, I was just the temp typist, so while I found this interesting, it didn't particularly bother me. I just kept typing.

Finally, I turned to the person sitting closest to me. "Hey, what's going on?" I asked.

"The Iranians just seized our embassy in Teheran," he said.

"Okay," I said and kept typing. Iran, after all, was not my problem. I was hired to type, not to solve international disputes.

Suddenly, George Merliss, executive producer of the show, flew into the room. Although he was a little Jewish guy with glasses, this morning he was more like General Patton. He began shouting instructions to everyone within earshot. "You! Call the White House," he commanded. Then he spun 30 degrees, and his finger was directed at someone else. "You! Call the Pentagon!" "You! Call the congressional leadership." Everyone in the room got an assignment. Boy, this was exciting.

Well, I wasn't expecting an assignment. I mean, I was a temp. But then Merliss was pointing at me! "You! Call the Islamic Center in Washington."

I started to explain that I was just a temp, but then I thought, well, okay. I mean, it's your $5 an hour. What do I care how you spend it? So I took off the headset and picked up the phone and dialed. The phone rang, and them someone answered it.

I thought this would be a good chance to put my education to work, so when the person answered the phone, I said in Arabic, "*Salaam aliekum. Ana min al-*Good Morning America."

Barely had I gotten the words out of my mouth when George Merliss, the excutive producer of the show grabbed me by the collar.

"You speak Arabic?" he demanded.

"Yes," I said.

"Where did you learn it?"

"When I lived in Iran."

He stared at me and said, "You lived in Iran?"

Well, I had been to Iran, and I had been alive, so that pretty much qualified as "living in Iran." So I didn't think that saying that was so bad.

Now, just to clarify things, Iranians don't speak Arabic, they speak Farsi. But at ABC News no one knew...or even much cared, for that matter.

"Do you know anything about these hostages?" he demanded.

"Sure," I said.

I mean, that was not really wrong. I knew that there *were* hostages. The guy sitting next to me had just told me that, so yes, technically I knew about the hostages.

"Can you write something?" he asked.

"Sure."

I could write that "there are hostages," so yes, I could write something.

"Get this guy a desk and a typewriter," he ordered, seemingly oblivious of the fact that I was already seated at a desk that had a typewriter.

And so it was that I was hired as a Middle East expert for *Good Morning America*, and my career in TV was started.

After this, we all went into a giant conference room, and all the big names at ABC News were sitting around a massive conference table, and a woman who was the senior producer pulled down a map of the world and took about five minutes of running her finger around the Middle East to find Iran.

No kidding.

In my first week there, anxious to please, I produced a massive "background paper" on how the CIA had overthrown the popularly elected Mohammed Mossadegh in the 1950s. This they found far too complicated for TV. Instead, they used to ask me questions like, "Is it Imam or Iman?" Stuff like that.

After I had been at ABC for about eight months, interest in the hostage story began to wane. So much so that the powers that be decided to let the "expert" go. But after such a heady experience, I found it difficult to go back to graduate school. Here, I had been surrounded by astonishingly average people, all making much more money than a full professor of history at Princeton and hardly working at all. And such a fun environment. So much action! TV was for me.

So far, so good. And all so easy!

But how to proceed?

I could see immediately that I needed credentials, which the Graduate School of Journalism at Columbia University was happy to provide...for a short nine-month course of almost no content and, of course, my $17,000.

When I graduated from Columbia, I got my first job in TV—as a "production assistant" on a public affairs TV show on WNET/Channel 13 in New York. Except that the job was in New Jersey.

WNET/Channel 13, New York's premier public television station is, ironically and through an accident of birth, actually licensed in Newark, New Jersey. And so, to protect the license, WNET opened a kind of Potemkin studio in Newark—a place to show that when it came to New Jersey, they were serious,...which clearly, they weren't.

The station produced a weekly public affairs show about New Jersey called *Mainstream*, which aired on Saturday mornings at 7 a.m. It was so terrible that even my own mother would not get up to watch the show.

The show was hosted by a minor New Jersey political figure named Tom O'Neill, who was about as destined to be a TV personality as I, at 5 feet, 6 inches, was destined to be an NBA all-star.

To make O'Neill better, the station sent him to weekly TV personality lessons at the Lilyan Wylder School in New York, where they tried to teach him to be an engaging personality. It was hopeless. But each week we could tell which lesson Lilyan Wylder had tried to drum into poor Tom O'Neill. One week it was "looking up," and throughout the half-hour talk show, O'Neill would bob his head as energetically as one of those bobble-headed dolls that people used to put in the back windows of their cars.

Another week it was "move your arms," and O'Neill did his very best impression of someone afflicted with Saint Vitus dance.

My job consisted of making coffee, slicing bagels, and photocopying scripts, all pretty scintillating work, almost as scintillating as the show itself. The set consisted of two swivel chairs, a potted palm, and a flag of New Jersey.

I began to wonder exactly what it was I had done.

Then, as luck would have it, Channel 13 decided to have an "election special." It was primary time in New York, and Channel 13 was going to produce a live two-hour special on primary night entitled, cleverly, *The Democratic Primary in New York*.

The candidates were Jesse Jackson, Walter Mondale, and Gary Hart. This was 1984. They were all in New York.

And the station, which, despite its $100 million a year budget, barely produced any television at all, had decided to go for broke and try a live two-hour special.

Now, what did that mean—*live two-hour special*—when produced by WNET/Channel 13?

Mostly it meant four swivel chairs instead of two.

And…Channel 13 was going to roll-in three videotape pieces…profiles of the candidates. Or actually, reports on what they were doing the night of the primary.

Now, Channel 13 was not really a news organization. It was barely a TV organization. The staff used to joke that the call letters WNET stood for "We're Not Exactly Television."

So everyone in the building was pretty freaked out over the two-hour special.

It would be produced by Joan Konner, who was then a senior vice president at WNET and would later become the dean of the Graduate School of Journalism at Columbia University.

In order to gear up for the "special," a big meeting was held one evening in room 435 of the main office of Channel 13 on West 56th Street.

Anyone who wanted to work on the "special" was invited to attend.

So I went. I made the commute from the New Jersey offices and went to the meeting. Maybe they needed someone to slice bagels?

There were about 50 people milling about the room as Joan Konner explained how the "special" would work.

The station was looking for volunteers to produce the three tape roll-ins.

Peggy Girshman, who later would run the science desk at NPR, was standing next to me. When the call came for producers, she poked me and said, "Put up your hand."

"But I never produced anything before in my life," I said.

"Do you think anyone here knows what they are doing? Put up your hand," she said.

So I did.

And I got chosen to produce one of the three videotape "special reports" for the show for primary night.

I would produce the Jesse Jackson spot for the "special." Peggy would do Mondale.

"Go down to the field shop and pick up a crew," Peggy said.

"What's the field shop?" I asked.

"It's where all the camera crew guys hang out," she told me.

And so I did.

I headed down into the bowels of the Henry Hudson Hotel on West 56th Street, a place I had never been before, and found the field shop. There were the video crews—cameramen and soundmen. And the crews could smell right away that I didn't have the vaguest idea of what I was doing.

They, on the other hand, had done this many times before.

They could have been nice. They could have helped me. Instead, they decided to have a good time.

Dale Vennes, cameraman, and Nick Pavichivich, soundman. To this day, I remember their names.

"Ah, Mister Producer," Dale said as I walked gingerly into the New York field shop. "Are you gonna produce the Jesse Jackson piece, Mister Producer?"

I nodded. I was like a virgin who had wandered into a bordello.

"What kind of lenses should we use here, Mister Producer?" asked Vennes.

Lenses? I had no idea.

"The regular ones," I said.

He turned to Nick. "We're going to be using 'the regular ones' tonight, Nicky." Pavichivich smiled.

They were like cats playing with a mouse before they eat it.

Nick and Dale decided that they would do only what I told them to do.

And who knew what to tell them? Not I.

So we went to the Hilton Hotel on Sixth Avenue, which was Jackson headquarters. As we pulled up in the WNET/Channel 13 van, another guy was starting to nose into the only parking space on the street. Dale hit the gas and cut him off.

The guy flew out of his car. Dale flew out of the van.

The guy started to yell at Dale, but Dale pointed at the plates on the front of the van. NYP 645.

"Do you know what NYP stands for?" Dale screamed in his face. "New York Police!"

The guy shrank, got back in his car, and sheepishly drove away.

Later I would discover that all the WNET cars had NYP plates. It stood for "New York Press."

Having found a good parking spot, Dale and Nick unloaded the gear. I tried to help, but I was told that that would be a union violation—touching the gear.

As soon as we were inside Jackson headquarters, Dale turned to me and said, "What should we shoot here, Mister Producer?"

Dogs can smell fear. So can cameramen.

"Shoot that," I said, pointing as something across the room. "And that. And that."

Not a clue.

"Anything else, Mister Producer?"

"And that."

I was trying to sound confident. Forget it.

And so we shot a bunch of stuff. And that, so to speak, was that.

And then we drove back to Channel 13 with the tapes. I had a deadline to meet. The live show was starting at 5 p.m.

I was assigned an edit room with Freddie Rodriguez as my editor. Freddie was a very nice guy, with a thick Puerto Rican accent. He had been editing at Channel 13 for years, and now he was sitting behind his massive editing room console—a vast array of switches and dials and buttons and screens—ready to go. It was so complicated that it looked like Mission Control at NASA.

When we saw the first footage of the Jackson piece, he swung around to me and said, "You sure you know what you're doing here, man?"

I had, of course, no idea. But I pressed on and gave Freddie instructions on what to put where. "Take the cut…now," I said, snapping my fingers. (I had seen this in the movies, but I had never edited a thing in my life.)

"You sure you wanna do that, man?" Freddie asked again and again.

And each time I gave him more instructions.

"Okay, man," he said, and pushed the appropriate buttons to make the screens light up, the decks whir, and the images flicker.

Meanwhile, downstairs in Studio 2D, the two-hour special had already started,…and I am still cutting the Jesse Jackson piece.

Soon, the phone began ringing in the edit room.

"It's Joan Konner," said Freddie to me, clearly unnerved.

"Where the hell is the Jackson piece?" demanded Joan.

"It's coming," I said, all bright and cheery.

Cut, cut, cut. Freddie Rodriguez was looking at me as if I were insane.

Cut there. There. Edit there. Take it.

"Okay, man," he said, and shrugged his shoulders.

Freddie Rodriguez probably had cut about 1,000 pieces in his life.

I had cut one—or about half of one—so far.

The phone rang again.

It was Joan Konner. She said, "Where is the piece?"

"It's coming."

We slammed it together.

Downstairs, the "special" was entering its second hour.

The producer had already run the Hart piece and the Mondale piece. She was swiveling in her chair.

I ran down the hall with the tape and entered into the big control room in Studio 2D, just like in the movie *Broadcast News*.

Everyone, everyone in the world, seemingly, was in this room.

There were maybe 50 people in there. Executives. Producers. On-air talent. At the center of the room, Joan Konner sat in a gigantic swivel chair all her own, kind of like Captain Kirk on the bridge of the *Starship Enterprise*.

Through the large glass windows, I could see the two-hour live "special," which was going on now, even as we spoke. But when I entered the room, all eyes turned on me.

I handed Joan the tape.

"Jackson?" she asked.

"Jackson," I affirmed and turned to go.

"Don't go anywhere," said Konner, and she put the tape into a playback deck next to her chair. She wanted to look at it before it went on the air.

Now, the piece I had produced ran about three minutes. But about 1 minute and 10 seconds into the piece, Konner hit the eject button, and the tape came out. She held it in her hands. Then she stood up, turned to me, and said, "This is the worst piece of sh*t I have ever seen in my life," and she threw that tape across the room.

It smashed against the Plexiglas wall.

This was not looking good.

The room was completely silent.

"Get out!" she screamed. "You will never work in this business again!"

I slunk out the door...my career a shambles.

The next day, I returned to slicing bagels, and I started to think about law school.

Three months later, Channel 13 was doing another special on the closing of Fort Dix. There was another big meeting in room 435 for anyone who wanted to work on it.

Of course, I went to the meeting.

"Who wants to produce for the Fort Dix special?" the man at the front of the room said.

My hand shot up.

"Wait a minute," said the executive producer. "Have you ever produced anything before?"

"Sure," I said, "for the election special."

"Oh, okay," he replied.

I was told to report to the field shop on Monday to pick up my crew. It was Friday, so I had a whole weekend to plan.

There was a movie playing called *A Soldier's Story*. It was the Denzel Washington breakout vehicle, and I figured, "It's about the Army, so I should watch this thing."

So I went to see *A Soldier's Story* over the weekend.

I saw it six times in two days.

And I took careful notes on how it was shot and edited.

Wide shot of the parade ground. Close-up of the flag. Close-up of the shoes. Guy with the trumpet. Back to the flag.

Shot by shot, I watched *A Soldier's Story*...over and over again, until I could see every shot in the film, one by one.

On Monday, I picked up the crew in the field shop.

Dale Vennes and Nick Pavichivich.

"Hey, Mister Producer," Dale said, somewhat amazed. "You still got a job?"

Clearly, they had seen the "election special."

We drove out to Fort Dix.

"What do you want us to shoot this time, Mr. Producer?" Dale asked me.

But this time I had an answer.

"Wide shot of the parade ground. Close-up of the flag. Close-up of the shoes. Guy with the trumpet. Back to the flag."

And he did just that.

We went back to New York, and I went into the edit room with Freddie Rodriguez.

"Hey man, you still working here?" asked Freddie, somewhat incredulously. He too had seen the "election special."

I also told him exactly what I wanted. "Wide shot of the parade ground. Close-up of the flag. Close-up of the shoes. Guy with the trumpet. Back to the flag."

I was making *A Soldier's Story*.

Except I was doing it at Fort Dix.

"Hey, man," said Freddie, with genuine warmth, "this is lookin' pretty good. You're cuttin' new ice!"

And when my segment was done, it looked just like *A Soldier's Story*, except in New Jersey.

And when I screened it for the executive producer, he loved it.

He loved it so much that my segment aired that night on the *MacNeil/Lehrer News Hour*, the national news show on PBS.

A Soldier's Story—except it was at Fort Dix.

And it was made by me.

And *that* was how I became a TV producer.

If I can do it, so can you. Trust me.

5

The Karma of Shooting

In the early days of film and television, video and film cameras were huge and weighed so much that you either had to prop them up on a tripod or hire a moose to carry them around. The moose was called the *cameraman.*

Today, your iPhone and most digital video cameras are light and tiny, so the way we work with them is going to change. There are some people who will stick an iPhone on a tripod that is about a hundred times the size of the phone. This I call insane. The small cameras give us an opportunity to reinvent what filmmaking is all about. We are going to work in a way that is much more natural and far simpler.

One hundred years ago, still photography also required giant cameras mounted on tripods. Photographers shot on sheet film, one exposure at a time. It was difficult work, and when subjects came in to be photographed, they had to stand or sit rigidly in front of the camera while the photographer, working under a hood, squeezed off a single static shot.

If you're like me, you probably have pictures somewhere in your attic of ancient relatives who were photographed like this. Your great great great grandfather is sitting rigidly upright, dressed in his best clothes. Photography was a serious business.

Then, in the 1930s, the Leica Company invented a small, handheld 35-mm camera. Suddenly photographers could dive into situations. They could move with ease. Photography became far more intimate, more alive. In fact, it became an art form in its own right. Great photo-journalists began to see and capture the world in a very different way. This was the photography of *Life Magazine*, of *Look*, and of *Magnum*. It was intimate and powerful.

Until now, "professional" television and filmmaking have been done the way 1890's photography was done: big, heavy cameras on tri-pods. And the results were the same. Look at the anchors on the *Evening News*. They look like your great great grandfather—dressed in a suit, sitting rigidly upright, humorless.

Our iPhones and small handheld video cameras are the Leicas of television and video. They allow us to create film and TV and video that are more powerful, more intimate, and much more interesting, not to mention vastly cheaper. But this means that we have to work in a different way as well. We can't just put the camera on a tripod and push the button.

I want you to think of shooting video as a racquet sport, like tennis. Instead of dragging around a giant box and camera, you're going to get "into play" with the action. You're going to move. You're going to be fast, agile, and responsive.

First, you have to dress for the sport.

A few years ago, I had a new hire come in for a reporting job on a local TV station I produce. All my journalists carry their own small cameras and shoot their own stuff. But this woman wanted to be a local reporter, so she showed up in a pencil skirt and gold stiletto heels. Wrong. I sent her home to change. Sneakers and comfortable clothes are best for this kind of work. We move around a lot—and fast.

As with any racquet sport, shooting good video is all about anticipating where the ball—or the action—is going to be and getting there first, as opposed to chasing it. If you're a good tennis player, then you'll know that the essence of the game is getting ahead of the ball. You don't want to chase it all over the court. You want to be in control. The same goes for video. And, as with any racquet sport, it's going to take some practice for you to get good at it. You will, but it takes time.

The first step in this life-changing process is getting to know your camera.

Your camera is not just some tool like a wrench. Your camera is a part of you—an extension of you—like a tennis racquet in the hands of a pro.

So, before shooting, I want you to do some shooting exercises—without a camera.

I want you to observe how you already "see" the world every day. You will discover that, like so much else in this business, you already know where to point the camera and exactly what to shoot.

I used to teach at Columbia University. Columbia is on 116th Street and Broadway in New York. Harlem begins at 125th Street and Broadway, just nine blocks north of Columbia. For many years, my students, most of them from out of town, would nervously make their way up to Harlem with their tripods and video cameras. Then they would produce their "documentary." I have seen this film about 500 times. A slow pan across 125th Street and a deep, pretentious voice saying, very slowly, "This...is...Harlem. The...heart...of...black...America," as the pan completes its wander.

Now, no one in their right mind walks up to 125th Street, bends over, and then slowly pans their head down the street. No one. We just don't look at the world like that.

If you went to 125th Street for the first time, how would you "see" the world? What would you see, exactly? The first thing you would do, most likely, is to see the whole street as a wide shot. Then, individual things would get your attention. A woman walking across the street. A group of kids. A car backing up. A couple walking. A changing street light. A series of stills. That's how you see 125th Street. Now, if you were to make a film about 125th Street, that is how I would want you to shoot it, because that is what a viewer would resonate best to—what he or she would see as well.

You see how easy this is?

So, before you even start to shoot, I want you to engage in a few exercises. I want you to walk out of your house. Go to some place you have never been before. If you can, have someone blindfold you and drive you there. And when you get there, I want you to observer how you observe the world. Write it down. Shot by shot. Do this a few times until you become cognizant of how you are already perceiving the world all the time. Then, when you are aware of what you already know, you are ready to start shooting and reproducing only that.

■ ■ ■ How to Hold the Camera

If you are shooting on an iPhone, grasp the phone by the edges, making sure not to block the lens with your finger. Then hold the camera horizontally at all times when you are shooting—never vertically.

This horizontal hold will allow you to match the aspect ratio of a TV screen. Vertical will only cut the picture—and the wrong way.

If you have a camcorder, it probably has one of those straps on the side that you slip your hand through to hold the camera.

Don't put your hand through the strap.

Putting your hand through the strap forces your elbow into a 90-degree angle to get the camera in front of your face. Hold a camera like this for more than a few minutes, and unless you are Arnold Schwarznegger, you are going to start to tremble. This is not a normal way to hold anything. Would you hold a baby like that?

Wrong!

In the early days of video, the cameras were so heavy that the only way you could carry them around with you was to hoist them onto your shoulder. This then became the "industry standard." Not for us. Instead, I want you to cradle the camera in both hands, gently, almost lovingly. Hold it in front of you. Now, when you are ready, bring it up before your eye. See how much more mobility this gives you. After you have taken the shot, relax and go back to cradling. See, no stress.

Right!

Now I want you to take your camera or iPhone with you and do the same exercise you just did, learning to observe the world, but this time, do it through the camera's lens. But don't record. We're not ready for that yet.

When it comes to your iPhone, you may want to hold it to shoot the way you hold it to make a call. Don't do that. The aspect ratio has to match. Don't hold it vertically.

Wrong!
Instead, hold it horizontally.

Right!

■■■ Starting to Shoot

■■ READY TO ROLL

For your first shoot, I want you to pick a relatively simple location. Someplace you are familiar with. Pick just one location. Pick someplace simple, preferably in your own hometown. Don't wait to make a big trip to Paris to start shooting. Any location works for these early lessons, and the easier the better.

We are going to make a short, one-minute video out of this first shoot. We're going to make a simple story. "This is Jack's Bakery. It's the best bakery in Westport, Connecticut." So let's keep the location simple as well.

Don't just go out on the street and start shooting at random. And don't start making a massive documentary about global warming or racism in America. Just keep it nice and easy and local.

■■ HERE ARE SOME GOOD PLACES FOR YOUR FIRST SHOOT

A local restaurant
A dog groomer
A bowling alley
A local jeweler
A nail salon
A barber shop
A tattoo parlor
A dentist
A veterinarian

These are the kinds of places where things "happen" all the time. This is all I want for this very first piece. Find one contained location where things "happen" (such as the ER, except that no one ever died in a nail salon—so far as I know).

What I don't want you to do is to use any relatives or family members. Don't shoot things at home. Don't shoot things that are outdoors. Don't do basketball games. We'll save that stuff for later.

We're going to make a one-minute video about your local restaurant, for example. This is not an investigative news story. This is not a feature film. This is just a simple, one-minute video about a local establishment—just the kind of video someone might put on his or her website, for example.

You can almost hear the narration now: "This is Bob's Pizzeria. He's been in business in Hoboken since 1987."

Get the concept?

How do you find your location? Just wander down the street and start talking to people. You would be surprised at how amenable people are today to being filmed. Everyone has a video camera. Just tell them that you want to make a small video about them and their place. Tell them that you are not with the Immigration and Naturalization Service—this will be your biggest problem! Tell them that you are not *60 Minutes*. This is not an investigative piece. Also, stay away from major chains such as McDonald's or Starbucks. They'll need corporate permission, which can take forever. Just select a small, friendly mom-and-pop shop.

■■■■ A Word About Rejection

We have all experienced rejection at one time or another in our lives, some of us more than others! As you enter the world of video and production, you are going to get rejected a lot. Don't worry about it, and get used to it.

I am not a big fan of "hidden cameras," and you should not be either. As you walk into any shooting situation, you want the enthusiastic cooperation of everyone involved. The more cooperative the subjects, the better the final product will be.

Don't be secretive. Be straightforward about what you want to do. Some people will be delighted to be on TV and to help you out. Others won't want you filming near them. Fair enough. If someone says the he or she doesn't want to be filmed, move on.

Many years ago I was in Kenya shooting some stories for *The Today Show*. I was doing a story about the Masaai. In order to avoid the influence of tourists, with the help of Angela Fisher, a long-time professional photographer in Africa, I found a Masaai tribe in western Kenya that seemed pretty unspoiled.

I arrived at the village and began shooting. No sooner had I gotten the camera out of the bag than the Chief approached me. Aside from his Casio watch, he was dressed entirely in Masaai gear.

"Three minutes, one hundred dollars," the Chief said, tapping his watch.

"Chief," I said, "I am here with NBC News." With a big emphasis on N-B-C. "You know. American TV?" I waved my arms in a big square to show a TV set. Of course, I thought, what am I doing? These people don't even have electricity. They live in huts made of straw and animal dung. What am I doing talking about NBC?

The Chief looked at me. Then he reached into his red tunic and withdrew a pile of business cards. "Everyone pays." He flipped through the cards. "CBS, ABC, BBC,...even...[and here he made squinty eyes] NHK Japan."

Well, I was a freelancer, and I didn't have the budget to start shelling out $100 for every three minutes of shooting. But I had to get started.

"Okay," I said, "one hundred dollars for three minutes. But...I want everyone to look at the footage when I am done."

The Chief clearly did not care. He counted his $100 and clapped his hands. "Okay, okay."

Suddenly, a dozen women, all in bright Masaai regalia, emerged from one of the huts. They lined up and started singing and dancing a "native dance." Wait a minute, I thought, I have seen this in *National Geographic*.

I shot the whole thing, and looking at his watch, the Chief clapped his hands and said, "Stop" when the three minutes were up. The women began to return to the hut.

"Hang on!" I said. "Everyone gets to look!" And I played back the three-minute tape for the village. Everyone gathered around. Although they had all been filmed by just about every major network in the world, no one, as far as I could tell, had ever taken the time to show them what they had shot.

They were delighted. They made me play it back a half-dozen times.

The Chief could see that there was mileage in this, so he invited me to come live in the village for a week, shooting whatever I wanted free of charge, so long as he could direct—which he did with great enthusiasm. He became a kind of Steven SpielNkomo. "Go back. He did not get the goat."

Now, you're probably not going to shoot in a Masaai village for your first few shoots, but the idea of "opening up the process" and sharing is a good one.

Once you've secured a location, you're ready to start shooting.

Here is what you *don't* do.

What I don't want you to do is just show up with the camera and start shooting everything and hoping for the best.

▪▪▪ What *Do* You Do?

When people get their hands on a camera, they get very nervous. They are afraid that they are going to "miss something." So they end up shooting everything. They collect a big pile of stuff and hope that when they take it back to the edit room, they will find something in it.

When Francis Ford Coppola made *Apocalypse Now*, he shot a ratio of 475 to 1. That is, he shot 475 hours of film for every hour you actually saw on the screen. Do you think this is expensive? You bet it is. Do you think it is time-consuming? To say the least. If you have a $100 million Hollywood budget, you can afford to work this way. My guess is, you don't.

When you go out to shoot, I want you to shoot almost nothing. Television and film are minimalist. A little goes a long way.

Think about it this way: You probably have written a great deal in your lifetime. When you set out to write 250 words on something, you don't start by writing 80,000 words just to make sure that you didn't miss anything and then edit it down, do you?

Nope.

You write what you need to tell the story you want to tell. You hear it in your head before you put pen to paper. Well, that's how we're going to approach making TV and video and film.

Minimalist.

Simple.

Easy.

Now, there are two parts to making a video—whether it's a reality show for cable, an informational video, or a feature film, it doesn't matter. There are always two parts:

- Acquisition
- Editing

Acquisition is the act of going out in the field with a camera and shooting all the raw material you will need to create the video. *Editing* is when you assemble all the material you have to tell a compelling story.

This week we are going to focus entirely on acquisition—the shooting part. Later we will edit what we shot this week.

Here's a great thing to remember: If you can shoot perfect video, the rest is easy. If your shooting is a mess, then the edit will be a disaster and a perpetual rescue operation.

So, before we do anything else, I am going to make sure that you can shoot perfect video every single time—and do it quickly and simply. It isn't so hard. In fact, it's quite easy.

Remember, I make only one demand: *perfection!*

From now on, everything you shoot is going to be perfect.

Absolutely perfect.

And here's why.

As I said before, if you take the camera out and shoot some video that is less than perfect, you have two choices: Either you can put the less-than-perfect video into your film and ruin your film, or you can throw out the less-than-perfect video you shot when you get home, in which case all the time and effort spent shooting it were, in fact, a complete waste of time.

The camera is in the palm of your hand.

You are in control.

You will decide when to push the "Record" button and when not to.

So, from now on, you will only push the "Record" button when the shot you see in the viewfinder is absolutely perfect. Otherwise, you are not going to push it.

"But I might miss something," you say.

This is true.

Also remember: *I want you to miss almost everything.*

We are going to become really minimalist shooters. From now on, we're going to shoot only exactly what we need and not one bit more. Like the movie *The Deer Hunter.* One shot. That's our goal.

Learning what to shoot will take time, but by the time this week is over, you will be an expert camera person, probably better than most professionals.

And here's the great secret: If you can learn to shoot cleanly and efficiently, the rest will take care of itself. No kidding. So this first week is really important.

■■■ Exercise Number 1

■■ IN THE RESTAURANT

If you watch at lot of TV, you'll see that there are a huge number of TV shows about food and restaurants. The Cooking Channel and the

Food Channel for sure, but there are food and cooking-related shows on almost every other channel as well. The Travel Channel has more food shows than it has travel shows.

Why is that?

First, as I mentioned at the beginning of this book, everyone eats three times a day, at least, so food is something we are all interested in.

Second, restaurants are easy places to shoot. All you have to do is show up. The rest just happens in front of you.

So, for our first exercise in learning how to shoot, let us pretend that we are going to make a one-minute video about a restaurant.

How do we do that?

The average restaurant is open for 10 hours a day, from the time the first delivery vans arrive to drop off the day's food until the last cleanup and lights out. Let's say that's 10 hours, or 600 minutes, of real-time events happening all day long.

Your job here is to extract from those 600 minutes of reality a single minute of video that will be both compelling and tell the story of the restaurant.

How do you do that?

First, let's think about how all this works. Here's the starting point:

600 minutes of "restaurant reality"

Now, you are going to go into that restaurant with your camera. I want you to shoot 20 minutes of material, from which we are going to cut a one-minute video for the web.

You are going to be shooting what we call a 20 to 1 ratio. That is, you will capture 20 minutes of raw material, but the viewer will only see the 1 minute we will make of this.

You are going to "harvest" 20 minutes of material from the 600 minutes or reality.

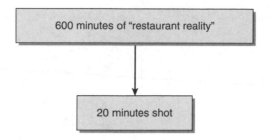

The 20 minutes is what you have "brought home."

The other 580 minutes you didn't capture has now ceased to exist.

This is a very important point: *If you didn't shoot it, it didn't happen.*

So, in this first act of shooting the video, you have effectively eliminated 97 percent of what happened in the restaurant. You have captured only 3 percent of the "reality." The other 97 percent has already ceased to exist.

So the decision of "what to shoot" is really, really important.

Of course, you could shoot all 600 minutes with multiple cameras. This would cost you a fortune. You would be screening and editing your raw material for months. And eventually, you would have to make the same decision about what to cut out. But you would have spent hundreds of thousands of dollars. Maybe you would have a future in Hollywood!

As you can quickly see, most of filmmaking is in deciding what "not to shoot" because that's 97 percent of what will have to do with your potential material. But first, let's look forward a bit. This is really interesting. Once you have shot all the material you will need, you're going to edit the 20 minutes down to the 1 minute that people ultimately will see.

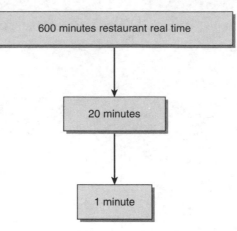

That one-minute video is *all* that your viewers are ever going to get to see or know of your experience in the restaurant. The rest simply does not exist for them.

So the 600 minutes of reality in the 10 hours of the restaurant at work becomes the 20 minutes that you have captured, thus losing 97 percent.

Then you are going to take those 20 minutes and edit them down to the 1-minute video that your viewers are going to get to see.

That's another elimination of 95 percent.

Only 5 percent of the 20 minutes is going to survive the cut.

Thus, in the end, your viewers only get to see 0.0016 percent of the reality you experienced in the restaurant.

For the viewer, 99.9984 percent is lost. Unknown. Forever.

You see why I said this is a minimalist business?

And you see why the little bit that you shoot, that 3 percent, has to be perfect?

Because we are really dealing with so little material, though, making it perfect will not be that hard. In fact, once you realize what a tiny world you are dealing in, it all becomes quite simple.

■ ■ Knowing What to Shoot—and What *Not* to Shoot

First, let's go to the restaurant. (Good plan so far.) And let's take our cameras.

When you arrive at the restaurant, however, I don't want you to touch your camera. Leave it alone for a good 20 minutes.

Instead, I want you to walk around the restaurant. Feel it. Smell it. Get a sense of the flow of the people and of how the kitchen works. Let the staff and the diners get used to you. You get used to them. And look around. Look around a lot. Take in all the things that the restaurant has. Observe what you observe.

Now is the time that you are going to get in touch with your deep instincts about what a film is supposed to be like. Remember, you have invested more than 30,000 hours getting ready for this, and only 10,000 makes you an expert.

I want you to walk around the restaurant, and I want you to observe what catches your eye. This is not about looking for shots. This is not about preinterviewing people. This is about having an experience and being aware of it. This is about figuring out what you want to shoot.

I want you to take a pencil and a piece of paper, and in those 20 minutes, I want you to write down seven events that catch your eye.

I don't care what they are. They will be different for everyone, but what do you see that makes you take a second and say, "Hey, that looks interesting"?

You are connecting with the shooting location on a very basic level. What are the things that grab your attention?

Did you ever see an old TV show called *Supermarket Sweep*?

It was first broadcast in 1965, but it also has had two revivals, the most recent on PAX-TV in 2001.

The idea behind the show was that three contestants were placed in a supermarket. Each one had a basket, and each had 1 minute and

30 seconds to race through the supermarket filling the basket with as much stuff as he or she could.

When the time was up, whoever had the highest total value of stuff in his or her basket was the winner.

Of course, the game had a basic flaw. To win, all one needed to do was to head for the meat counter and fill the basket with filet mignon. Simple. But not everyone did that. Some had a technique of running through the canned goods section with an arm outstretched knocking the cans into their basket as quickly as possible.

When you go to the restaurant with your camera (or anywhere else to shoot, for that matter), you are playing video "supermarket sweep."

You have one minute to gather the most valuable shots you can find because that's all you're going to be able to show to anyone in the final product anyway. So head for the filet mignon, and ignore the milk.

For today's exercise, I'm going to ask you to shoot 12 minutes of raw material—no more, no less. Later, we're going to cut our first one-minute video out of that.

Now, if you had a limited amount of time to run through the restaurant and capture only the most valuable, the most interesting material—only the stuff that really caught your eye and made you take a moment and say, "Jeez, that's interesting," what seven "events" would you shoot?

What really catches your eye?

■ ■ PEOPLE COOKING FOOD

The kitchen is where all the action is, and if you were free to wander around any restaurant, my guess is that the kitchen is where you would find the most exciting events. This is why so many TV shows take place in and around a kitchen, from *Kitchen Nightmares* to *Iron Chef.* It's instinctive.

Those steaks on the grill with those flames shooting up into the sky. The chef bent over the frying pan sautéing the fish. Those are real eye-catching events. People cooking food is the number one answer in shooting anything in a restaurant. It's where you are naturally drawn.

If people cooking food is the number one event that catches your eye in a restaurant, what is the second most popular event? If you're like most people, it would be *people eating food*. Take a walk around the restaurant. What catches your eye? People eating.

Third? Pouring the drinks?

Waiters serving the food?

Washing the dishes?

The maître d' seating people?

The chef yelling at the waiters? (Tension in the kitchen!)

The staff grabbing a smoke out back?

People talking to each other at the tables?

The hostess searching for a reservation?

A whole table singing happy birthday?

Someone mopping the floor?

Setting up the tables?

Food trucks arriving?

Someone uncorking a bottle of champagne—with a nice pop.

Okay, I asked for 7, and now we have 15. Fifteen interesting things that go on in a restaurant you might like to shoot to tell the story of the restaurant in one minute.

Want to add anything else?

Got enough here to make a pretty rocking one minute if we shot it well? I think so.

More than enough.

If you could shoot all these things and shoot them all perfectly, would you have all you would need to make a great one-minute video?

I think so.

Now notice what you did not say (and I have done this exercise hundreds of times).

You did not say, "Shoot the exterior of the restaurant."

Let's be honest here. Unless you went to film school and you failed to "forget everything you know or think you know," no one ever says, "Shoot the exterior of the restaurant." In film school, we would call this the *establishing shot*.

And why does no one ever say, "The exterior of the building really catches my eye"?

Because it doesn't. Because it's boring.

Let's say that in real life I told you that you must go and try lunch at Bouley Bakery, a restaurant in Tribeca in downtown New York.

You are incredibly hungry, so you get in a taxi and speed off to the Bouley Bakery.

Boy, you are so hungry that you could eat the taxi seat.

When you finally pull up at the Bouley Bakery, what do you do? (And you only have one minute!)

You jump out of the cab and tear into the restaurant at fast as you can.

You don't jump out of the cab, cross the street, and gaze on the facade of the restaurant, tilting your head upward slowly and then from left to right.

No one does that! So why would you drag your viewers there when you shoot the piece? If you don't want to see that, what in the world makes you think that your viewers want to see it?

They don't.

Like you, they just want to get into the restaurant.

So take them there.

See? Instinct.

So, from now on, no more exteriors unless the building is by Frank Gehry.

Also, you will notice that you did not mention, "Shoot an interview." No one ever does.

Again, why?

Because interviews are boring!

Let's be honest. They are boring. No one wants to see them.

If you were just arriving at the restaurant, you were ravenously hungry, and you only had one minute, the last thing you would want is some annoying maître d' stopping you and saying, "Hey, before you eat, let me tell you how I got into the restaurant business."

You would shove that guy out of the way. You are hungry! And you only have one minute!

No one wants to see a talking head on a video. No one. And no one wants to see the outside of a building (unless it's done by some famous architect and is really eye-catching). So you know what? Don't waste your time shooting them!

Nothing screams "change the channel" better than starting with an exterior shot followed by a talking head. Nothing screams "this is going to be really boring" better. So don't do it.

Just don't do it.

Follow your instincts about what to shoot. Your instincts, honed by 36,000 hours of practice, will not fail you. Learn to trust them.

Okay.

Now that we have figured out what seven events to shoot, how do you shoot them?

Take out the camera and turn it on.

Keep it in automatic. Trust me.

■ ■ ■ The Five-Shot Rule

Now, let's go back to following your instincts.

What is the number one event in the whole restaurant that caught your eye? Where was it the most interesting? If you could show your best friend only one thing in the restaurant, what would it be?

My guess is that it would be the action in the kitchen.

So now, camera in hand, walk into the kitchen.

Instinct!

And there is Chef Lisa, busy cutting the carrots.

Where does your eye go?

To the action.

And right now, where is the action? Where does your eye naturally lead you?

To Chef Lisa.

Good.

Watch her for a minute.

Note where your eye goes naturally.

It goes to her hands as she cuts the carrots.

This is where the action is centered. You can't help but be drawn there.

So this is your first shot.

This is what your instincts are already telling you.

Good.

Now where does your eye itself come to rest? What is the thing that calls for your attention?

Again, just go with your instincts.

It's the hands. Actually, it's the action of the hands chopping the carrots.

So this is going to be your first shot.

A close-up (CU) of the hands.

Now, I want you to shoot this thing perfectly. Don't be shy. Video and film are no place for the shy. So, leaving the camera in wide (W) view, I want you to shove that camera in there and fill the frame with a really beautiful shot of that silver knife slicing through those orange carrots. Get as close as you can. Be aggressive!

There is no point in holding back in the fear that you might annoy someone or get in their way. There are two people in the kitchen with jobs to do—Lisa's job is to cut the carrots. Your job is to film her doing that. If you hold back and stay far away, you will get bad video. You may run it with the legend underneath: "This video is terrible, but at least I didn't annoy anyone." You may win "Most Congenial," but you also will win "Most Likely to Be Unemployed."

I want this to look like the most expensive commercial that the National Carrot Alliance has ever paid for. And you can do it. All you need is the scene and you shooting high-definition (HD) video. Fill the frame. Find the perfect shot. You are going to live and die by your work, so do whatever you have to do to make sure that you have the perfect shot. Once you have the perfect shot in your viewfinder, and only then, hit the "Record" button. Hold the camera perfectly still. Do not move the camera while you are recording. Don't move it an inch. Don't move it a millimeter. Don't move it at all. Hold your breath and count to 10 to yourself: "1,...2,...3,...4,...5,...6,...7,...8,...9,...10.

Okay, breathe.

Hit the "Record" button again to stop recording.

Congratulations!

You've made TV.

Okay. Now, here is where your instincts really pay off. Here is where all those 36,000 hours of study are going to come into play.

The act of shooting video is more than just shooting video. Eventually, that video of the silver knife going through the orange carrots—that CU of the hands in action—is going to be on a screen. People are going to look at it. This is the whole reason you are doing this.

If the very first shot your viewers see is a CU of the hands in action, then what is the next shot they are going to want to see?

Go with it? What is it? What would you expect to see after a CU of the hands? Dig deep into your 32,000 hours of learning.

A close-up of the face!

Of course.

By showing the hands, you have raised a question in the mind of the viewer. Okay, ... whose hands are these?

Now you must resolve that issue. Your eye naturally goes to the face, without even thinking about it.

So do that with the camera.

With the camera still in pause, find an equally beautiful shot of the face—a CU as the chef chops the carrots.

When you have the perfect face shot, hit "Record" again. Count to 10. *Do not move the camera while shooting.*

Fine.

Now you have two lovely shots—a CU of the hands and a CU of the face.

Again, follow your instincts.

If the first shot is a CU of the hands and the second shot is a CU of the face, what do your instincts tell you the next shot is going to be? What do you, yourself, *want* to see?

You want to see the wide shot (WS), the one that puts together the hands and the face. So now, with your camera paused after the

10-second shot of the face, find the perfect WS showing all the action, hands and face together.

When you have that perfect shot, hit the "Record" button again, and once again count to 10. *Do not move the camera while shooting!*

Okay.

Now you have three shots. A CU of the hands, a CU of the face, and a WS of the whole. You are working on a sequence. Now think of two more angles of attack you can take on the chef cutting the carrots.

Come on....

Yes, an *over the shoulder* or *point of view shot*. Get behind the chef, point the camera over her shoulder, and show me what she sees as she cuts the carrots. Find the perfect shot. Don't do anything until you have the perfect shot. Take your time. Now, when it looks so painfully beautiful in the viewfinder, hit "Record," count to 10, and *do not move the camera while you are recording.*

Good.

Now, one more shot. One more angle to record.

This one will be from the side. Okay?

So, once again, move around until you have the perfect shot of the chef still chopping the carrots from the side. Hold. Hold. Now hit the "Record" button, and *do not move the camera while you are recording.* Count to 10.

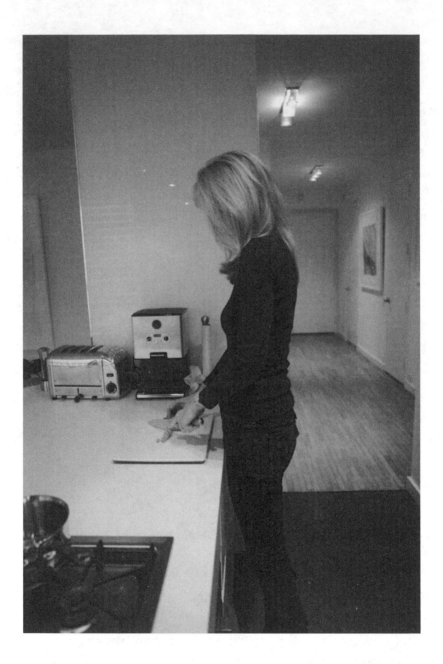

Good.

You are done.

You have shot your first sequence.

■■■ Five Shots

A CU of the hands
A CU of the face
A WS
An over the shoulder shot
A side shot

Each shot is 10 seconds long.

The camera doesn't move.

Well done!

See how simple that was?

Now, that's fine for a chef in a restaurant, but let's change the story.

Now you are in Florence, Italy, doing a documentary for The Travel Channel. You have gone to the Ponte Vecchio in the center of Florence, and there in the very center of the Ponte Vecchio is a small leather shop. But this is not just any leather shop. This leather shop is where the very best shoes in Italy are made, by hand. Each pair takes a week to make and costs more than $2,000. This will make a good story.

As you enter the shop, what catches your eye? Where does your eye go as the old shoemaker works on a pair of very expensive shoes?

It goes to him, hammering away on the heel.

And where exactly does your eye go?

It goes to his hands driving the nail into the heel.

So what is your first shot going to be?

A CU of his hands.

Good. Don't move the camera, and hold for 10 seconds. Pause.

Now, if a CU of the hands is your first shot—a beautiful CU shot of those nails being driven into the heel of the shoe with the thwack, thwack, thwack of the hammer as it strikes the nail with great force and concentration—then what is your next shot going to be?

Instinctively?

A CU of the shoemaker's face—his face concentrating so deeply on driving home the next nail perfectly.

A CU of the hands.

A CU of the face.

And now?

A WS.

Then over the shoulder.

Then the side.

Fine.

Totally new story.

Now you are in Antwerp at the most famous diamond cutter in the world. And you are doing a video for Harry Winston Jewelers. And the company is paying you a fortune for it. And it's all about diamond cutters.

So, as you stand in the small shop and the master diamond cutter is tapping away at a 25-carat diamond, where does your eye go first?

That's right.

A CU of the hands.

Then a CU of his face.

Then a WS.

Then an over the shoulder shot.

Then a side shot.

Five shots.

Like always.

Okay.

New story.

Now you are in Geneva, Switzerland, where you are doing a video for the website for Piaget, the watch company. Did you know that Piaget's Emperador Temple watch sells for $3.3 million? The company can afford to spend a bit on its video, but this has to be good. You have gotten complete access to the assembly of one of these watches, and before you, the master watchmaker is busy putting in the balance wheel. It is very detailed work, and he is hunched over his workbench, deep in concentration. Where does your eye go?

To the detailed work of his hands.

First shot—CU of the hands.

Second shot—CU of the face.

Third shot—WS.

Fourth shot—over the shoulder.

Fifth shot—side.

Five shots.

Now you are back in the United States. You have made so much money from the Piaget and Harry Winston gigs that you can afford to make a documentary about heart transplants for PBS. The film is called *Transplant: The Clock Is Ticking*, and today you are actually in an operating room at Mt. Sinai Hospital in New York, where you are filming an actual heart transplant.

You are all gowned up, but you have been given access as you observe one of the world's greatest transplant surgeons close the chest of her patient. She has just started the new heart. Now she is standing over the patient, stitching up the chest. She pulls the needle and thread though the incisions, closing it.

Your eye goes to her hand, tracing the needle through the wound.

CU of the hand.

Then CU of her face.

Then a WS.

Then an over the shoulder shot.

Then a side shot.

Ten seconds each.

Do not move the camera while recording.

Are you starting to see some kind of pattern here?

No matter what the story, no matter what the circumstance, the shots are all exactly the same.

CU of the hands—10 seconds.

CU of the face—10 seconds.

WS—10 seconds.

Over the shoulder shot—10 seconds.

Side shot—10 seconds.

In all cases, *do not move the camera while shooting. Ever!*

If you do this, and nothing but this, you will have a perfect film every single time.

Hard to believe, no?

But it works.

I call this the *five-shot method*, and it is absolutely foolproof.

This makes the "work" of shooting remarkably easy.

All too often filmmakers and videographers fret over "how to shoot" a particular scene. They agonize. They get overwhelmed. They hire directors. The five-shot method ends all that agonizing. All you need to do is attack every situation with this (you can add a few shots later, but for now, don't deviate!), and you will be absolutely fine.

Why does this work so well?

Video and film are a language.

And like all languages, they have a grammar.

In the ancient past in this country, people studied grammar all the time. It was the foundation of language. Then, about 40 years ago, the formal study of grammar disappeared from most schools, ironically at about the same time that television became our dominant medium.

Now, most people learn to speak English not by rules but rather by listening to what "sounds good."

A few years ago, I set out to learn classical Arabic.

Within a week, the professor told us that in some cases we should use the subjunctive and in others the nominative.

I had no idea what he was talking about, having never really had a formal education in English. So, before I could really learn Arabic, I had to go and buy myself a basic English grammar book and learn how grammar worked for English. Once I had mastered that, Arabic was much easier, and so, ironically, were French and Spanish.

Film and video are languages, and as such, they also have a grammar, even if most people learn how to make TV and film the way they learned to speak—by watching and imitating.

That is fine, but you will never really get a good command of Arabic if you don't learn the grammar. By the same token, you will never get a good command of video and film if all you do is look and imitate.

These five shots are the building blocks of the grammar of film and video. Like the noun, verb, pronoun, adjective, and adverb, they can be endlessly ordered and reordered to "say" pretty much whatever you want to say to your audience in an elegant and coherent way.

But you must start by acquiring the "building blocks"—the five shots—by making sure that they are the best and most beautiful shots you can create, and this requires discipline.

Great shooting and great filmmaking are not the result of wildly waving the camera around and getting as much as you can and later rescuing it in the edit. This is a mess—even if it is how most films and videos are made. It is undisciplined and wrong. And it will always leave you trying to save a pile of junk in an edit that will be long, tedious, and painful.

However, if you follow the rules I have set before you and stick to those rules rigorously, you will always make a great success and sometimes even a great film. And it will be incredibly easy.

One last note; above all else, this is the most important single piece of advice I can give you. If you follow nothing else, you must follow this. When you are shooting, *do not move the camera* when recording.

Ever.

No moves.

No pans.

No tilts.

No zooms.

Nothing.

In film and video, motion is in the edit, not in the camera shooting. I want the shooting to be extremely disciplined. Pause between each shot. Take your time. Wait until you have the perfect shot in the viewfinder—then hit the "Record" button. Count to 10. Don't move the camera.

Often, in the classes, this notion of "don't move the camera" causes a lot of dissention from those with prior experience. So here is what I do to make the point. I tell my students to go to YouTube and watch the famous shower scene from the Hitchcock movie *Psycho*. You know the one I am talking about?

In people's minds, it is filled with action.

If you watch the scene, really watch it shot by shot, that is, you will see that it is all stills. Hitchcock never moves the camera.

If you want to get really good at this, download your favorite film, and call out each time there is an edit. CU of the hands. CU of the face. Over the shoulder shot...and so on. Don't take it from me.

The way to make a great film is all around you. All you have to do is know how to look.

If you can do this, and nothing but this, you will make a perfect film every single time.

■ ■ A NOTE ON THE MATH

Sometimes people will say, "Seven events, five shots, right? So all I need is 35 shots." Not exactly. An "event," like cooking food, means everything that goes on in the kitchen. So five shots of cooking the steak, five shots of making the salad, five shots of slicing the bread, and five shots of plating the food. Get the concept?

■ ■ ■ A Word About Interviews

Here is how really bad filmmakers make a film: The first thing they do is sit down with the subject and interview him or her for an hour or so. Then they shoot some cover material they call *b-roll* to cover up the sound bites in the film. Then they lace together the sound bites and connect them with narration. Then they cover the whole thing with the b-roll, hoping that some of the stuff matches what the person is talking about.

This is a great way to make an absolutely unwatchable video or film, and it happens all the time.

You will notice that in the five-shot method, there are no interviews. It's designed that way. In real life, unless you work for the FBI, you never "interview" anyone. This is not how people deal with the real world, and it's not how you should deal with capturing the real world.

Instead of interviews, I want you to get into the practice of capturing a few *sound bites*, that is, bits of conversation that you have with the subjects of your film. This is very different from interviewing.

Let's go back to Chef Lisa cutting the carrots.

You are standing next to her as she slaves away at cutting the carrots. While shooting her, you have developed a kind of relationship with her, a kind of intimacy. Now, as you watch her cutting the carrots, you feel an urge to ask her a question. It's the kind of question you might ask whether you were carrying a camera or not. I call this, the *question that begs to be asked.*

So ask it.

Once you have completed the five shots, turn the camera on her and say, "Don't you ever get tired of doing this?"

She'll appreciate it.

She'll look at you (and your camera and thus also your viewers) and say, "I hate every minute of this stupid job."

And *that* is your sound bite.

That is all you want or need.

Nothing more.

Now, when you go to edit your film together (which we are going to talk about next), your sound bites are "nested" in the film. That is, they were captured visually at the moment of reality.

How many times have you seen a film or TV show where you are shown a lot of action or activity or reality, and then, suddenly, you are shifted back to a "talking head" in a chair. Back and forth, back and forth—from the reality to the chair to the reality to the chair. It can make you seasick.

No more. From now on, your sound bites are going to be recorded at the moment of reality and then edited into that moment. Do you see how much simpler and more elegant this is?

So, when you go out to shoot, I want you not only to get your 12 minutes of footage, but I also want you to acquire three or four sound bites. No more.

■■■ Calma: The Story of Mario Biasetti

Many years ago, I took a job with Time Warner. The company was thinking of starting a 24-hour business channel to be called *Time Warner News Service* (TWNS). The idea behind it was to follow the global stock markets on a 24-hour basis, London to New York to Tokyo, and drive a television business channel around it.

In order to "sell" the concept to the board at Time Warner and thus unlock the hundreds of millions it would take to create such a channel, the company had hired a man named Reese Schoenfeld to produce a five-minute demo video that would show what the channel would look like. Reese Schoenfeld had been the first president of CNN.

The demo was going to have two anchors at a desk in a newsroom, and they would cut to some sample business stories from around the world. Schoenfeld hired me to produce the sample business stories.

For me, this was a fantastic opportunity; a chance to be on the very ground floor of what could become the next CNN.

"For the first piece," Schoenfeld told me, "I want you to go to Bahrain and make a 1:20 [that would be 1 minute and 20 seconds] news story about the oil business."

Well, that didn't seem too hard.

"And I want you to stop in Rome and pick up a cameraman named Mario Biasetti. He's the best in the business."

Well, fair enough. It had been many years since my days with Dale and Nick, and to work with the "best in the business" would make my life infinitely easier.

I flew to Rome to meet Mario. He was a thin, wiry, athletic 60-year-old cinematographer who had been "in the business" for many years. He knew his stuff, or so I had been told. We also would be accompanied by his extremely attractive 22-year-old female assistant. Italian film directors!

Biasetti brought with him about 1,000 pounds of camera gear—tripods, lights, monitors, and the biggest betacam video camera I had ever seen.

And needless to say, this was expensive. Biasetti was not cheap, and neither were the business-class tickets he demanded, nor the first-class hotel. However, Reese said that he was the best of the best, and who was I to argue? My only prior experience had been as a producer at CBS News. I was anxious to work with a "real" pro.

When we finally got to Bahrain, our schedule allowed us only one day of shooting, so I wanted to make it a full day. As a good producer, I prearranged a very full schedule of shooting events to make sure that I got everything I needed to cut the 1:20. These were the days before I figured out the five-shot method, let alone anything else.

On arrival, we were picked up by our limo and taken to our five-star hotel. We left the hotel very early the next morning to catch the brilliant sunrise over the gulf. We were at the Bahraini waterfront in plenty of time to film the sunrise, and Biasetti soon had his betacam set up on a tripod on the dock. I stood by as the red sun rose over the sea. Arab dhows were raising their sails. The muezzin was calling from the mosque: "Allah. . . . Akbar." It was perfect. I could see lots and lots of stuff that I wanted to get—or rather that I wanted Biasetti to get for me.

The only problem was that Biasetti was not shooting anything. Instead, he was a good 20 feet away from the camera, moving around the docks, looking at every scene through a kind of frame he made with his index fingers and thumbs.

Try it yourself. Point the thumb and index finger of your left hand to make a long L. Now do the same with your right hand. Now, with one hand facing inward and the other outward, join them together in front of your face.

Did you get a perfect rectangle?

Now, start to view the world through it.

Voila!

You're a professional director.

I call this the *Hollywood square.*

Personally, I found this annoying. I didn't need Federico Fellini. I needed a cameraman. This made me crazy. Time went by. The sun was coming up. Women in veils walked by, men in thobes. But not a frame of video was shot. Mario just kept walking around looking through the box between his fingers.

Finally, I had had enough.

"Hey Mario," I yelled, just to get his attention. He looked up at me, clearly annoyed.

"Roll tape Mario!" I yelled, clapping my hands to make sure he got the message. "Roll tape!"

He looked at me over his black reading glasses. "Stupido Americano," I could hear him thinking.

"Calma," he said. "Calma." And went back to looking for shots through his four-finger frame.

More time. More looking. More fingers.

Then he moved the camera on its tripod a little to the left. Finally, I thought. But, no. More looking, More framing.

"Mario! Roll tape! Roll tape!"

Again, over the reading glasses, with that look of utter contempt: "Calma...."

His assistant just sat in the corner smoking a Gitane and reading the latest issue of *Elle*. She wasn't going to be of any help.

Finally, after a seemingly interminable time, Biasetti pushed the "Record" button. You could almost hear the capstans turn as he started to roll off tape—30 seconds, 40 seconds. Then he stopped.

He stepped away from the camera and began walking around making his little box with his hands again. The camera stood, untouched. The assistant lit up her second Gitane.

I felt myself going slowly insane.

We had been on the waterfront for the better part of an hour, and so far he had shot about 30 seconds of material. I had laid out a whole shooting schedule for the day, and we were already far behind. If this was how this great Italian cinematographer worked, I wanted no part of it.

Finally, after moving the camera for what seemed the hundredth time, he touched the "Record" button again. Twenty seconds. Stop.

This is how the day progressed. We went to each of the locations I had prebooked: the oil fields, the loading platform, the ministry, downtown. But no matter where we went, it was always the same. He spent a great deal of time looking but almost never shot anything.

And no matter how much I yelled or screamed or beat him, he refused to roll tape until he was ready, and he always gave me the same answer: "Calma."

But I was not so calma. Time was running out. I had only a one-day shooting permit. Surely, I had believed that we could accumulate enough material in one 12-hour day to cut a video that was only 1 minute and 20 seconds long. But clearly I was wrong. I had not accounted for Mario Biasetti.

By the end of the day, Mario Biasetti, the great Italian cameraman, had shot perhaps 20 minutes of tape. Total. Total!

We were done.

And I was screwed.

How could I go back to New York having spent so much money and time, having flown all the way to Bahrain, having taken Biasetti and his assistant and myself 12,000 miles, not to mention the five-star hotel, the limo, the meals...and show Reese 20 minutes of footage?

What kind of idiot does that? I would fire myself.

My job with Time Warner was over before it had started.

I was agitated on the flight back to New York, and I didn't sleep at all when I got home. The only thing to do, I thought, was just get the whole ugly mess over with.

Reluctantly, two days later, I dragged myself over to Reese's office to deliver the bad news and hand in my resignation.

I got there early in the morning, and there was Reese. He was a big man with a big, toothy grin.

"How did it go?" he asked me, all smiles.

"That guy Mario," I said, "is a moron! He only shot 20 minutes for the whole day. No matter how much I yelled at him or beat him, all he said was 'Calma! Calma! Calma! Calma! Calma!' This is a disaster!"

Reese looked at me for a minute.

"Have you looked at the tape?" he asked.

I had not. In those days you needed a separate beta playback deck, and I didn't have one. But Reese had one in his office.

"Let's look at the tape," he said, and proceeded to put the one tape I had managed to bring home in the deck. He hit "Play."

We watched as the tape rolled.

Every shot was perfect. Every one.

Perfect.

There was nothing on there I did not want to use. Or could not use.

Mario Biasetti had given me a tape with a 1:1 ratio. It was like looking at a coffee table photo book entitled, *The Oil Business of Bahrain.*

Stunning.

Shot after shot.

My biggest problem now in cutting a 1:20 piece out of this raw material was having to lose 18:40 of equally beautiful material.

Now, that experience taught me a very valuable lesson. One that is almost as important as *don't move the camera.*

And that lesson is: *Calma!*

Calm down.

Relax.

Breathe.

Then calm down some more.

When we go out into the field to shoot, we are not there to shoot live TV. We are there to capture a few select moments and to capture them extremely well. As you know, you really only need 0.0016 percent of what you are seeing and experiencing in a day.

When people get a video camera in their hands, they tend to get hysterical, fearful that they are going to "miss something." When you go out to shoot this week, I want you to miss almost everything. But when you do shoot, I want you to really take your time and give me the most beautiful few shots you can make.

6

Week 3: Tell Me a Story

This week you're going to learn how to take your shooting skills and turn them into video stories that will attract and hold an audience, no matter what the topic. We are now about to enter the third week of your video life-changing experience.

Last week, I taught you how to shoot perfect video every single time, no matter what the subject, and to get a few sound bites. This will work whether you are making a 1-minute video for the web or a 90-minute feature film.

This week I am going to teach you how to take that material and make it into a great story every time.

Let's go back to our figurative restaurant. You should have seven small packets of sequences for each of the "events" you decided to shoot:

Cooking food.
Eating food.
And so on.

Each of these should have been shot with the *five-shot method*. And you should have two or three *sound bites*.

You should have 20 minutes or so of material in all.

Now we are going to distill this down to a very enjoyable and watchable one-minute video. And we are going to do it with a process that is repeatable every single time.

How are we going to do that?

Let's begin with the material that you shot.

COOKING	EATING	WASHING DISHES	PAYING THE BILL	POURING DRINKS	SETTING TABLES
	S1		S2		

Each of these *silos* now contains a number of sequences, all nicely shot in 10-second five-shot sets. No camera moves. There are also two sound bites that you have picked up along the way, each one marked by an *S*.

This is your *content*.

These are the building blocks from which you are now going to create your one-minute video.

How do you proceed from here?

Instead of having a written script, we are going to do this with no writing whatsoever. No pencils, no paper, no pens, no word processing, no nothing.

I want you to get your hands dirty in the video. I want you to reach in there and pull up the video you want and mess it around—craft it like clay.

Did you ever see the movie *Minority Report* with Tom Cruise?

You know the scene where he starts manipulating images in the air in front of him?

One day, in the not too distant future, that is how we will be able to edit films and video. We aren't there yet, but we are close enough that

that is how I want you to start to think. You are going to start manipulating the images and sounds that you shot.

How do you do that?

You have to start thinking of the story you want to tell with the video as a kind of "totality." In other words, you need to ask, "What is this all about?" before you can even get started.

So here is what I want you to do.

I want you to arrange the events you shot before in the order in which they are going to appear in your film or video.

This is not about choosing shots. And it is certainly not about writing a script. It's not about narration, and it's not about sound bites. It's about *what happened*. What, in the macro sense, is the story that *you* want to tell?

This is actually going to be very easy for you because, although you may have never written a script before, you have been telling stories your entire life.

Let's say that you woke up this morning after a particularly bad dream. (Mine always involve being homeless, but that's just me.)

In any event, you turn to your spouse or partner or whomever, and you say, "I just had the weirdest dream." And he or she says, "Tell me what happened."

And you say, "Well, first, I was on this plane that was going to crash, and then, suddenly, we hit the water, and I had to swim about a hundred miles. Then, while I was doing that, my mother came by in a rowboat. But she refused to pick me up unless I changed my shirt. And I explained that my shirt was back with the plane. And she said, 'Well, you better go back and get it because I am not taking you into my boat looking like that.'"

Ever have that dream?

Okay. You have the one where you are flying. We'll do that another time. For now, let's stick to this one.

So, when you are explaining what happened in the dream, even if it doesn't make much sense, you are telling a story. A simple story. First this happened, then this happened, and then that happened.

This is storytelling, and it's something you already know how to do.

What I want you to do now is to arrange the "events" that you shot in week 2 into a coherent "story."

First this happened, then this happened, and then that happened. As with the dream, you don't worry about sound bites or shots or narration. Same here. Just lay it out for me in as simple a form as you can, event by event.

So you might say: "Okay. First, there are the people eating, then the people cooking. No,...wait. First, it's pouring the drinks, then people cooking. Then people eating."

You can move stuff around as much as you like.

Eventually, you are going to get to an *order of events*. This works whether you are making a 1-minute video for the web, which is what we are doing here, or a 90-minute feature film. It's all the same. First this happened, then this, then that.

When you have finally got it in the order you want it, we are going to freeze it. We are going to commit to this as the "story I want to tell." We are going to call this *picture lock*.

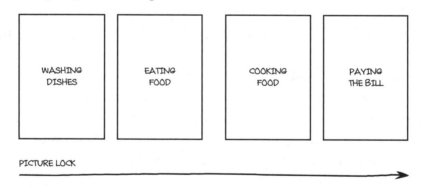

You don't have to use all the material you shot. In fact, as you will recall, you are going to lose 95 percent of it.

Once you have your picture lock in place, you may now proceed to the sound bites.

As you will recall, you recorded two short sound bites when you were shooting. Now, where do you want to put them? You can put them in anywhere.

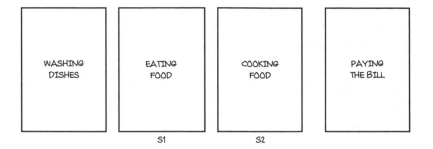

Okay.

Now you have all your sequences in order and your sound bites.

Here is where you have to step back for a moment. You have been very close to this film or video. Maybe you have been working on it for a day. Maybe you have been working on it for six months. Whatever the case, you are about to show it to someone who has absolutely no idea what you are talking about and a very limited attention span.

So now you have to put yourself in their shoes.

You have to stop now and look at this as someone who has no idea what this is about.

Here is where you are going to have to "tell me the story." Narrate it to me. Tell me what happened.

This is the *narration*.

This is where I need you to tell me the story in the simplest way possible. Don't be cute. Don't be artistic. Just talk to me.

And when you do this, we are going to lay the narration out exactly where it belongs as the story proceeds.

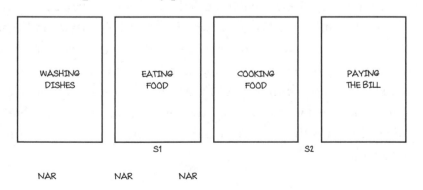

Good.

Now, do you know what you have here?

A *script*.

A script for the digital age.

No paper.

No pencils.

But the whole script.

That's it.

Done. See how simple that was?

Now let me show you something even cooler.

Let's look at the digital script we just made because it is something more than a digital script.

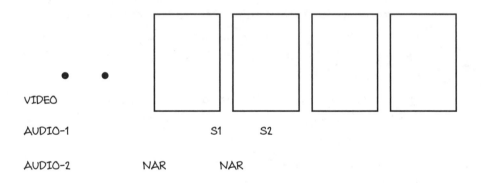

VIDEO

AUDIO-1   S1   S2

AUDIO-2   NAR   NAR

This is also the timeline for any nonlinear editing system. The top is the video track, and below that is located the two audio tracks.

So your nonlinear editing software—whether it's Avid or Vegas Video or FCP, it makes no difference—is also a script-writing tool. And from now on you are not going to take your video, transcribe it into text, write a script in text, and then change that back into video. As you can see, that would be crazy. Instead, you are just going to build the final film directly on the timeline using the timeline as a script-writing tool.

And the great thing is, when you are done "writing the script," you are also done editing.

See how simple and elegant this is?

7

Fluffy May Die

If you want to get people's attention and hold it with your videos, you have to do more than just point the camera. You have to tell them a story. Great filmmaking and great videos are about great stories and great storytelling.

When you learned to shoot, all you really had to do was to follow your instincts. You already knew what it should look like. When it comes to storytelling, you also already know how to do this. You just didn't know that you knew until now.

You have, in fact, been a storyteller all your life. The only difference is now you have to learn to do it with video. But it's much easier than you think.

Let's take a hypothetical example.

Let's say that instead of going to a restaurant to make a short video, you went instead to a dog and cat hospital.

So far, so good.

And while you were there filming, a little girl came in, clasping "Fluffy," her little dog.

And Fluffy has been hit by a car.

And the little girl comes in, tears in her eyes, cradling the dog, and says to the vet, "Mister, can you save my dog?"

Pretty good so far, huh?

And right before your eyes, with your camera recording, the veterinarian grabs Fluffy from the little girl's arms, puts Fluffy down on the table, and immediately begins to operate.

Now, because you are aggressive, as I told you to be, you wedge yourself and your camera between the vet and the dog, and you are able to get some really spectacular pictures of the dog lying on the table, its eyes wide open, panting and crying a bit, and fighting for its life while the doctor works. Fantastic! Unbelievable!

You got some really great footage there, all shot exactly as I told you to do it. Sequences. You never moved the camera. You got two sound bites.

The good news is that you had this fantastic experience and you have all this great footage and a great story to tell.

Now, the bad news.

The bad news is that you are in a very bad relationship at home.

Very bad.

You have been living with this person for about a year, and it is just not working out. I am sure that you have experienced this at some time in your life, so you know exactly what I am talking about.

There is lots of tension in the room.

You want it to work out, but you just don't know how to make this person care about you or love you or even really think about you anymore. He or she always seems distracted. He or she always seems to have something else on his or her mind. Let's call your soon-to-be ex "Pat."

So, you have been living with Pat for about a year, but things are really bad. You're almost at the end of the road, but you don't want it to end. Pat does.

But maybe, if you show Pat some of this incredible footage, somehow Pat's heart will be softened toward you. I mean, come on, "Puppy lives!" What could be more heartwarming than that?

So, as soon as you get home, all excited from your day of shooting, you say, "Pat, you won't believe what a day I've had. You have to look at some of this footage!"

But Pat is not interested.

Pat is busy texting someone!

So you get more aggressive.

"Pat, you have *got* to see some of the footage I shot."

You get Pat's attention for a moment.

"What?" Pat asks.

"Pat, I want to show you some of the footage I shot today."

More texting.

"What?" Pat asks again.

Now you are getting annoyed. You slam your hand down on the table.

"Just look at one shot, Okay? Just one lousy shot!"

Now you have Pat's attention. Pat knows that soon you will be dividing up the DVDs and stuff, and Pat does not want to annoy you.

"Okay. Show me one shot."

Here's your opening.

What one shot do you show Pat, since this is all that Pat will ever look at?

Do you show Pat the exterior of the dog and cat hospital?

I don't think so. I don't think you have much chance of getting Pat's attention with that one.

No.

You show Pat your very best shot. The one shot that will melt Pat's heart and make Pat say (in your mind), "What an idiot I have been" and maybe start to cry.

And what is that "very best shot" (when you only get one chance)?

Why, it's that close-up of Fluffy on the table, wide-eyed and whimpering, as the vet begins to try to save her life.

Killer, killer shot!

You don't really have a choice.

What else would you show?

Now, if you are going to show soon-to-be-out-the-door Pat the shot of little Fluffy fighting for her life, what must you show your viewers as the first shot?

Let's put it this way: The viewers at home have even less of a relationship with you than soon-to-be-history Pat.

You didn't go to the Bahamas with the viewers.

You didn't have that fantastic time in the back of the car with the viewers.

The viewers could not care less about you.

You could be on fire, and the viewers would walk away.

So, if you're going to show Pat that killer shot when you have only one chance, then you have to show your viewers the best killer shot as your first shot. Because if you can't get their attention from the very start, they will be gone before you can say, "Stand by...more to come." You will be talking to no one.

There is a natural human instinct to save the good stuff for later. Call it the *squirrel syndrome*. We like to save things for later.

Don't do that.

If you don't reach out and grab someone from the very beginning, there will be no later. No one will be there to see what you have been saving up.

In a recent survey, 40 percent of people who watched online video dump out in the first 10 seconds. This means that you have 10 seconds to get their attention—maybe less. Ten seconds to reach through the screen, grab them by the throat, and say, "Hey, pay attention. This is interesting."

And you have only one chance to do that.

So you have to use your most exciting shot as the opening shot. You have no choice.

Here's the secret to success every time.

It's all about the first shot.

If you pick the first shot and then "let the story go where it wants to go," you will have a great piece every single time.

When I say "let the story go where it wants to go," as opposed to where you might want to take it, you probably don't know what I mean...yet. But you will. Stick with me.

Now, remember when I said that you have to let the story go where the story wants to go? Okay. Here's what that means.

Here's your opening shot: Fluffy, wide-eyed and frightened, fighting for her life.

FRAME-1

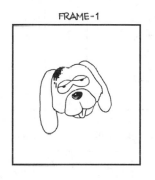

FRAME-1

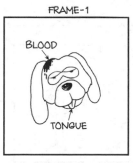

FLUFFY THE PUPPY WAS HIT
BY A CAR ... AND MAY DIE!

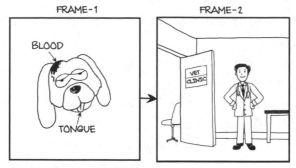

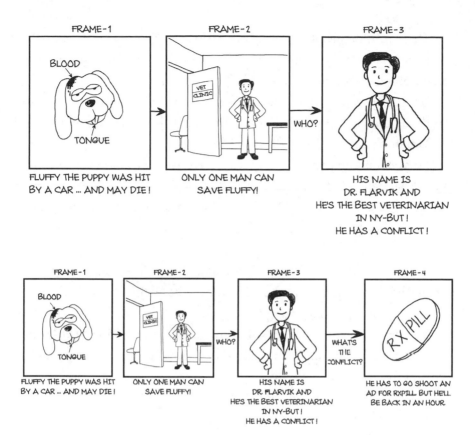

Now look at that shot.

Is anyone turning away from that shot?

I don't think so.

So you have everyone's attention—at least for a moment.

That's pretty good.

Now, here's the interesting part.

What is the average person thinking when he or she looks at the video of little Fluffy, wide-eyed and whimpering, on the table?

What goes through the average person's mind?

They say, "What happened to the dog?"

It's what everyone says.

That's pretty amazing.

Three million people all over the world are watching the first opening shot of Fluffy fighting for her life, and they are all thinking the same thing at the same moment: "What happened to the dog?"

It's pretty cool, when you think about it. Three million human minds all lined up asking the same question at the same moment.

You don't get that every day.

So you now have no choice. You have to answer their question, "What happened to the dog?" You have to.

So you say, in narration, "Fluffy the dog was hit by a car and may die."

Is anyone changing the channel?

I don't think so.

Three million people are now all hanging on the Fluffy story, all asking the same question at the same moment: "Will Fluffy die?"

Once again, you have no option.

You have to answer the question, so you say in narration, "Only one man can save Fluffy" (and you have a long shot of some guy dressed in white at the end of a long hall).

Is anyone changing the channel?

I don't think so.

Three million people all over the world are all asking the same question now at the same time: "Who is the man?"

And once again, you have no choice. You have to answer the question.

So you say, "His name is Dr. Flarvik, and he's the best veterinarian in New York,...but he has a conflict."

Three million people. Anyone tuning out? I don't think so.

And once again, you have no choice. You have to answer the question: "What's the conflict?"

So you say, "He would like to save the dog, but right now he has to go and shoot an ad for Rxpill, but he'll be back in about an hour or so."

Okay.

This is not a script. This is a dialogue. You are in a "conversation" with the viewer. You put up a picture, the most powerful picture you have. They ask a question, you answer the question, they ask another question, you answer the question, back and forth, back and forth, to the end of the story.

You see how much more compelling this is than writing a script that you then try to jam down someone's throat?

Now, what makes this so simple is that you have been doing it all your life—telling stories. Having conversations.

This is how we explain things to our husbands, our wives, our parents, our children, our friends and coworkers.

Well, you know what? The people you are making your films and videos for *are* your friends, your family, and your coworkers. They are people just like you, and they want to be told a story just like you would tell it to them in person.

So, you see, you already know how to do this.

You have been doing this all your life. You are more of an expert on storytelling than you already are on television and film!

Now let's go back to our hypothetical.

This time, you are married to Joe. But now it's a very happy marriage. Very happy. And Joe is a partner at Goldman Sachs. Last year Joe brought home about $40 million. (It was not a great year, but it was okay.)

You live on Fifth Avenue in Manhattan, and you don't have a care in the world. You have never worked a day in your life. Your entire life is spent having lunch with "the girls" and shopping. Occasionally, you attend a charity function.

Life is pretty good.

But yesterday was a bad day.

Mrs. Rodriquez, the housekeeper, was out sick. Again.

And your cat, Mr. Scruffles, had a cold and had to be taken to the vet.

So you had to cancel lunch and take Mr. Scruffles to the vet by yourself.

And while you were in the waiting room at the vet's, a little girl came in with a puppy that had been hit by a car.

And right before your eyes, the veterinarian saved the puppy. Amazing!

Now, you are not a filmmaker. You have never touched a camera, and frankly, it's the furthest thing from your mind.

But still, what you saw was interesting.

So, when you come home and see Joe at dinner, you have an interesting story to tell.

And across the dinner table, Joe says, "How was your day?"

And you say, "You'll never believe what happened to me."

And Joe says, "What?"

And you say, "I was at Dr. Flarvik's office with Mister Scruffles, and suddenly this little girl came in with a dog that had been hit by a car."

And Joe says, "Wow! What happened then?"

And you say, between forks full of pasta, "Well, I thought the dog was going to die, but Dr. Flarvik put her on the table and began to operate right there."

"Wow!"

You are telling a story.

It is something you have done your whole life.

You are also spinning out a script.

A compelling script. This works.

Now, if you had come home and Joe had turned to you and said, "How was your day?" and you had sat up ramrod straight in your chair and said, "More than 2,500 dogs are hit every week in the greater New York area. Fluffy was one of the lucky few," Joe would have said, "I think you have to dial back on that Prozac."

Because normal people don't talk like that.

No one wants to hear that. It's not normal. In fact, it's alienating.

But that's how people write when they "write for broadcast."

Constipated.

So I don't want you to do that.

I don't want you to "write a script." I want you to *tell a story*—something you already know how to do. You have been doing it all your life.

You see how simple this is?

This is not about "script writing." This is about *storytelling*.

So now just take the most powerful shot you have, the one that grabs your attention, and start with that. Then ask, "What does the average person think when he or she sees this?"

And you are off.

Let the story go where the story wants to go.

And now you know what I mean.

8

Week 4: Welcome to the Revolution

This week you're going to learn how and where you can start to sell your new skills!

After three weeks on the program, you now know how to make pretty much any piece of video you want. You know how to craft and tell great stories in video. As long as you stick to the rules, you will have an easy time, no matter what the subject matter. And the more you do this, the easier and more fluid it will become. But even now, you have all the basics. If you can make a compelling minute, you can make a compelling hour.

Later, in week 5, we'll talk about some advanced techniques, but you already are better than most professionals in the business, and you are now members of a fairly elite club: the video literate.

Television is the most powerful medium the world has ever known. Billions of people get their information and entertainment from it every day and devote a good portion of their lives to watching it. Yet, while billions of people watch television daily, the content that is on TV is made by an infinitesimally tiny percentage of those billions of people—a tiny self-elected elite that decides what "the rest of us" will get to watch.

When you think about it, it's kind of crazy.

We like to talk about a "free press," but what kind of free press is made by a tiny handful of people *for* everyone else?

If we ran the world of books and literature the way we run the world of television and video, then every book or newspaper in the world would be written by about a dozen people, and no one else would even think of writing a book or expressing an idea. We would never accept that, yet we readily do with TV and video.

We accept it because until now, the very act of making TV, video, or film has been so complicated and so expensive that no one could afford to try it on their own or even think about it. As a result, very few of us ever became adept at making video.

Now, thanks to an explosive shift in technology, suddenly, and virtually overnight, the power to create content that used to be restricted to the very elite few is open to anyone who wants to learn and try. If you have gotten this far, this now includes you.

Congratulations!

But what does this shift in the "power to create content" mean?

We are on the cusp of a massive change in the way that the media business works. You can see it all around you. Massive changes can be upsetting to the established order but also a fantastic opportunity to make a fortune if you position yourself correctly as the applecart of society is overturned.

Becoming video-literate is your first step toward putting yourself in a winning slot for the future.

If we want to understand where all of this is going to end up, then perhaps the best guide we have for the future is to take a look at the last time the arrival of a new technology unleashed a massive change in the world of media.

To do this, we have to go back about 500 years. But it's going to be worth the trip, trust me.

■ ■ ■ The Gutenberg Story: How One Simple Piece of Technology Changed the Entire World

Let's imagine, for a moment, that instead of living in the twenty-first century, you are living in fifteenth-century Germany. The odds are that you would be a serf. That is what just about everyone did for a living.

You spend your days milking the cows and gleaning the fields.

And you live in a hut. You share it with animals and about 20 other people, some of whom are relatives. Your bed is a simple affair of straw and insects. You take a bath about once a year, if you're lucky. You never brush your teeth, which fell out when you were about twenty anyway. And food? Well, let's just say that this is an era long before anyone even thought about sushi, let alone refrigeration.

There are no electric lights, no TV, no radio, no books, no photographs, no advertising, no department stores, no malls, no stores of any kind, no cars, no place to go, no travel, no schools, no education, and no one knows how to read or write. There is, in short, not much of anything. All the markers of a culture that we take for granted today do not, in fact, exist.

There is, however, the Church. And that is pretty much all there is.

And if you are willing to take a long pilgrimage—I mean walking hundreds of miles—there is a stained-glass window you can look at.

Get the picture?

Life, in short, is brutal, nasty, and dirty.

All in all, even with the pilgrimages, it is probably not exactly the life you had in mind.

So let's imagine that you are unhappy.

Very unhappy.

You are tired of the cows and the manure and the wheat gleaning and the witch burnings and wearing the same rags every day.

You are 24 years old, and you are having a midlife crisis.

But you're trying to deal with it.

You're talking to the priest.

And making lots of confessions.

You're beating yourself regularly until you bleed.

But one day (and one day is pretty much the same as the rest because clocks haven't even been invented yet), your wife turns to you and says, "Honey, what's wrong. You seem so unhappy."

You look at her, and suddenly, you can't hold it in any longer.

You crack.

And you spill your guts.

And you tell her that you hate your life together, you hate the hut, and you hate the cow. You hate the whole serf thing. It all feels some-how...wrong.

You are one lucky serf. Your wife is supportive. She gently strokes your head and says, "Well,...if you could be anything you wanted to be in life, what would you be?"

Now here's something you have not really thought about all that much. I mean, your father was a serf, so was grandpa, and so was his father before him. It's sort of been a family tradition going back a long time. But since she is asking, and since she looks so cute today, and all three of her teeth are that nice, radiant yellow, you decide to open your heart and be honest.

"Well," you begin, "if I could be anything at all,...I always...wanted...and I know this sounds dumb, to be either a...clinical psychologist...or a writer."

She smiles. Her face is blank. It's always blank, now that you think about it.

"What is a clinical psychologist?" she asks.

It doesn't matter. In fifteenth-century Germany, there are not a lot of jobs for clinical psychologists. But you can be a writer.

But to become a writer, first you must become a priest.

That's just how it is.

So, after much thought, you leave your wife, you take your vows of poverty and chastity and celibacy, and you join the priesthood.

And pretty soon you are wearing long black robes and swinging burning embers and hearing confessions all day long and sleeping on cold stone floors. Pretty good, huh?

After a few years as a priest, though, you become a monk. Well, not a full monk, at least not at first. No, first you must become an assistant monk, then an associate monk, and then a monk. Then maybe even senior monk, senior managing monk, executive monk? Who knows? The sky's the limit!

Then, after a few years in the monk business, the other monks come to you and say, "Brother Tom [this is your name, by the way], we have decided to make you a writer!"

Hot dog!

All the years of suffering and struggling and "paying your dues" are finally going to pay off.

You are finally going to become a writer!

So, with much ceremony, the other monks take you up into the tower. Up those long, narrow, cold stone steps you have dreamed of for so many years. Up to the *scriptorium*—the secret room where all the writing is done.

And there it is.

At long last.

The scriptorium.

At the top of the long winding stone staircase is a room filled with wooden desks. The scriptorium. And at each wooden desk, there is a Bible chained to the desk. And a monk sits at each desk and painfully copies the contents of the Bible into a bound vellum book, letter by letter, page by page.

And the senior executive monk takes you to *your* desk!

(Your desk! Pretty soon you'll have funny cups and pictures of the kids.)

And you sit in front of your pile of vellum pages, and the head monk opens the chained Bible and says, "Okay Tom, now we want you to take this pen and copy the Bible exactly as you see it, letter by letter, word by word, page by page. And be sure to draw in all those nice pictures of angels and cherubs."

So this is writing.

I mean, this is writing in the fifteenth century.

"Now Tom, we expect you just to copy exactly what you see here in the Bible. Don't go getting all 'creative' on us," says the senior executive monk with a kind of weird smile.

You nod. "No, of course not."

"Because Tom, we have been in this business for a thousand years. We have an 88 percent market share and 92 percent penetration."

"Impressive," you say.

"Yes. And you know what the 'Good Book' says...."

You pause and smile. You have no idea what he is talking about.

"If it ain't broke, don't fix it. Ha, ha, ha!"

You laugh along.

Well, what's the difference? Now you are a writer!

Congratulations!

And writing a book is a long, hard, expensive proposition.

First, writing, as it turns out in the fifteenth century, is a team activity. It takes lots of monks to write a book. And it takes about a year to do a really good book. And books are expensive! And there is a whole support staff at the monastery. There are ink fillers and researchers and associate monks and bookers and even receptionists.

Not to mention all that laborious and time-consuming handwriting.

"Man, if they ran credits at the end of the Bible," you joke to the monk sitting next to you, "it would add another hundred pages."

But no one laughs.

Oh well. In any event, now you are a member of the elite. You are a writer.

So now you're going out. You're dressing all in black—very downtown. And girls come up to you at parties (or witch burnings, or beheadings, or feasts of the virgin) and say, "What do *you* do for a living?"

And you say, with a smile, "I'm a writer."

They are breathless. Are you someone famous? Have you written anything I might have read?

And you look at them. This is soooo good.

"Ever hear of . . . Exodus?"

"Exodus?" they ask, even more excited.

You gaze off. Maybe you pick at a fingernail. "Yeah. . . ."

"You wrote *that*?"

"Yeah."

"Wow! We *love* that. With the burning bush and the plagues and all that stuff. So cool! I can't believe you wrote that!"

"Yeah."

"Wow!"

You pause for a moment.

"Hey, I've got a new book I am working on right now. It's called Deuteronomy."

"Dood-er-onemy? Weird name," they say.

"Oh, it's cool. It's all about laws and families and stuff. Kind of like John Grisham meets *The Sopranos*. You're gonna love it."

"When is it coming out?" they ask.

"About twenty years." You pause. "Hey, I've got a key to the scriptorium. Would you like to come up and . . . take a look?"

Really, life could not be better.

And the Bible?

Continues to be a big seller. Number one for years. Also, in fact, numbers two, three, and four. In fact, it's pretty much the only book in town.

But then, one dark day, a terrible thing happens.

Johannes Gutenberg appears.

With his printing press.

Gutenberg!!!

And he drags his printing press into your courtyard and yells up at your window, "Hey monks!"

And you all rush to the window and look out.

That jerk.

But Gutenberg is busy running his little printing press.

Bang, bang, bang.

And he holds up a sheet of paper.

"Look at what I got," says Gutenberg. "A book! And I made it all by myself!"

That idiot. You really hate this guy.

And you all rush downstairs to take a look at his "book."

"Oh Gutenberg," you say, looking at what he has just printed. "This isn't a book! No golden letters, no cherubs, no angels. Look at this man! This is terrible. Who is going read this thing? Look at this technical quality. Terrible! This isn't how a book is made. Writing a book is a group activity. You need researchers and associate monks and assistant monks and senior monks, and it takes years, pal. You can't just crank 'em out on that printing press of yours. No way!"

And all the other monks gather around you and back you up.

"You tell him, Brother Tom," they say.

And you're feeling pretty good because, after all, this is how books have been made for 500 years at least, maybe a thousand (who knows?). And a million monks can't be wrong, can they?

But you are wrong. They can.

Because in 50 years, (which is like an hour in fifteenth-century time), the monks and their monasteries are reduced to museum pieces. And your hand-written books are collector's items. And what is worse, the whole world you knew—the whole world, kings, priests, monks, and serfs—comes to a crashing halt.

Because of Gutenberg and his printing press.

This little piece of technology will bring an entire civilization to a close. This little piece of technology will prove more powerful than any king or pope or army or religion.

Because Gutenberg didn't just invent a cheaper way to make Bibles. He invented a way for anyone with an idea to get that idea published.

Now *that* was revolutionary.

Of course, that wasn't Gutenberg's plan. All he wanted to do was make some money from cheaper Bibles.

And any venture capitalist in fifteenth-century Germany would have run the numbers and seen that the new technology of the printing press completely changed the basic business calculus of the Bible printing business. Because now you could produce a Bible—which used to take a year and a whole army of monks—in just a few days with only one person.

Mass production!

Literally.

So even though Gutenberg and his backers sincerely believed that they had cracked the nut of cheaper Bibles, the real revolution was in what the printing press could do that no one could have foreseen.

The printing press suddenly, and without much warning, allowed anyone—anyone at all (and this is a very, very radical concept for fifteenth-century Europe)—to publish anything—anything at all— any time they wanted. The printing press was not really about cheaper Bibles. It was about the ability to disseminate ideas on a mass scale— and to send those ideas to everyone.

Sound familiar?

Now anyone with an idea, any idea, could do just that.

It was a very radical concept.

It was the Internet of its day.

And like the web, it turned the world of Medieval Europe upside down.

Today we live in a world dominated by television and traditional media.

And the contemporary world of TV is very similar to the world of hand-written Bibles into which Gutenberg was born. It is expensive to make TV, and the industry is controlled by a small and elite "priesthood."

But all this is going to change.

Your iPhone and the web make it possible for you to "publish" your work in video on a par with anything CNN or NBC can do—and at a far lower cost or complexity.

Your iPhone is the Gutenberg's printing press of the twenty-first century. It makes it possible for you to publish whatever you want, whenever you want, and in video, the lingua franca of our age.

The Gutenberg revolution went on to topple every major institution in Europe and later the rest of the world. The structure of religion, society, the economy, and the state; the nature of interpersonal relationships; the nature of entertainment and communication; and people's own perceptions of themselves. All that would change because of this one seminal piece of technology.

On August 3, 1492, Christopher Columbus left the city of Palos, Spain, and sailed westward across the Atlantic in search of a shorter route to China. Columbus' geography may have been off—he believed the circumference of the world to be a good 10,000 miles less than it actually was—but his luck was with him. On his way across an infinite and endless ocean, he bumped into the continent of North America.

Now, other Europeans had been to North America before Columbus. Most notably, Leif Eriksson, the Viking explorer who "discovered" both Iceland and the poorly named Greenland, before ultimately striking out and "discovering" North America in AD 1000. Yet the Norse discovery of North America goes far beyond simply an accidental landing. Thorfinn Karlsefni, who no one has ever heard of, actually headed a first colony in Vinland, as the New World was then called. In AD 1010, Karlsefni, who had married Gudrid, widow of one of the sons of Eric the Red, set out with three small ships and 160 men to settle Vinland.

Does the story sound familiar? Three small ships? Karlsefni?

Probably not, but there's a reason.

The Karlsefni settlements and Eriksson's discovery clearly predate Columbus by nearly 500 years. Yet the Viking discovery and subsequent settlements led to nothing. It was a sterile event in human history. It remained a sterile event because most people never found out about what Eriksson had done.

Eriksson lived before Gutenberg.

Columbus lived after Gutenberg.

And that made all the difference.

The first thing Columbus did when he got back to Europe was to publish. Eleven editions were published in 1493 alone. Six more editions were published in 1494–1497.

The work was disseminated in Spain, Italy, France, Switzerland, and the Netherlands.

Perhaps the most noticeable impact of the new print revolution was in the very name of the continent and the country. Although the New World was discovered by Christopher Columbus, it was not called "Columbia," which has a rather nice ring to it (this is now solely the name of a suburb of Washington, DC). Rather, the country and both continents were called "America," after explorer Amerigo Vespucci.

"Strange that broad America must wear the name of a thief! Amerigo Vespucci, the pickle dealer at Seville," wrote Ralph Waldo Emerson in 1856. But the fault was not Vespucci's but rather Martin Waldseemuller's. Waldseemuller was a cartographer who published *Cosmographiae Introducto* on April 25, 1507. It was one of the first atlases ever published, and as such—and since it was a printed document in mass distribution—it carried enormous weight.

Ironically, Waldseemuller, who was a clergyman, not an academic, who simply had a passion for maps and a printing press, decided to change his mind and not credit Vespucci with the new world. It was too late, however. Once the atlas was in print and distributed across Europe, Amerigo stuck and does so to this day.

One is forced to wonder what impact the printing press might have had on the world had it been introduced at an earlier time in history. What, for example, would the world be like had the printing press been invented in 1215, when the British nobility forced King John to sign the Magna Carta, relinquishing his power over the purse to Parliament. There was only one Magna Carta, and it is unlikely that very many people in the thirteenth century actually read that document.

Thus, in 1517, when a hotheaded young priest named Martin Luther got the idea that the Catholic Church in Rome might not be running things exactly the way he thought they should be run, he didn't get mad. He wrote it all down.

It was called "The 95 Theses," and according to the legend, he nailed it to the door of his church in Wittenberg. But Luther did something far more revolutionary—he published.

Within a few years of his writing down his list of complaints, more than 100,000 copies of the Lutheran doctrine were circulating in Europe. And they were circulating not in Latin, the language of the Church, which almost no one could read or write or even speak. They were circulating in Spanish, French, German, and Dutch, the languages of average people.

And what Luther had written made sense to the people who read it. So much sense, in fact, that they left the Catholic Church of their youth and joined in a revolution that overthrew the most basic and fundamental power structure in Europe, one that had been in power, quite literally, for a thousand years—the Vatican.

They did it because they were convinced by the *power* of Luther's *words*. Written words.

The power of the written word, the impact of Gutenberg's printing press, was so powerful that within only a few years of its invention, the machine itself overturned an entire culture and ended a way of life that had dominated Europe for almost a thousand years.

Every major institution was changed in an entirely fundamental way: the Church, the monarchy, the economy—even the way that people came to think of themselves.

With the arrival of the printing press, this one piece of fundamental technology turned the entire world upside down. We moved, as a culture, from being a society based on oral traditions to one based on the "written word."

Prior to the printing press, almost everyone in Europe was illiterate, sometimes even kings. After the printing press, the notion of illiteracy for anyone in power became unthinkable.

But the changes were even far more fundamental and far more profound.

The Church, which was once based on the "word of God" and found its power in an illiterate membership and a priesthood with direct access, through their Latin Bibles, was suddenly and violently transformed into a Church based on the "written word." As millions of people suddenly got Bibles in their own hands and could read the "word of God" for themselves for the first time, the whole nature of the Catholic Church and of how Christianity functioned underwent a fundamental shift.

And of course, the printing press, which now could crank out anyone's ideas to a newly receptive and literate mass audience, was suddenly replete with hundreds of variants on topics of religious discourse. And the once monolithic Church of Rome is now split and split again as Lutherans railed against Calvinists, against Baptists, and so on ad infinitum. The multiplicity of printing presses and opinions begot the multiplicity of sects and schisms.

In politics, the results were no less dramatic. A nobility that once felt secure in its ability to rule, granted by God and carried out through the "word of the king," now found itself increasingly under fire from the same source. Endless tracts on the "rights of man" begin to appear, and the entire notion of monarchy ultimately would be brought under scrutiny and collapse. All that would take time, though. In the shorter run, the notion of rule by the "king's word" was replaced by the "rule of law" or, more properly, the "written law," which everyone could see and read equally.

The Constitution of the United States is the perfect Gutenbergian form of government—a government based on a written, printed, multiple-copied document that everyone is free to read and know. The American society, at least to date, is entirely derivative of a "print-based" culture. It is not for nothing that the very first amendment of the Constitution deals with freedom of the press. It says, "Congress shall make no law abridging freedom of the press." We are a culture deeply tied to a fundamental piece of technology.

Wow!

Wasn't *that* something?

And all from the invention of the printing press.

Now, just think for a minute, what the democratization of video and television is going to do to our society.

And now, you have a ringside seat.

In fact, you're a player!

9

Week 5: Your Pathway to Success

This week we're going to expand on your skill set and begin to introduce you to even bigger and more lucrative markets.

Jack goes to Paris with a video camera. He shoots the most beautiful and well-lit video of the exterior of the Eiffel Tower that anyone has ever seen.

Does anyone want to look at this? Probably not.

Is anyone going to pay Jack for this?

Probably not.

Great videos of the exterior of the Eiffel Tower are a dime a dozen on the web—and for free. The last thing the world needs is yet another one.

Lisa also goes to Paris with a video camera, but she finds a very interesting small café off the Boulevard St. Germain. The café is owned by a fascinating woman who was once the prima ballerina with the Bolshoi Ballet in Moscow. On a tour to Paris in the 1970s, she met and fell in love with a young French filmmaker who, alas, was married at the time.

Are you starting to get more interested in this story?

I think so.

And how important is Paris?

Not very, although it does provide a lovely background.

Now you are starting to see the secret to success not only in film, TV, and video but also in any kind of storytelling.

It is all about the characters and the story.

There is nothing more deadly than a "documentary" about "an issue." Great stories are about compelling characters. Even "important" stories are still about characters. And in many ways, the smaller and more personal the story, the more compelling the larger story becomes because the more easily a viewer can relate to it. This is important!

If you ever read Pulitzer Prize–winning stories from, say, the *New York Times*, the subject matter might be welfare reform, but the story always will begin, "Mary Smith is a single mother of eight...."

If you can get the viewer to care about a person, that viewer also will care about the story. It is much harder to get people to care about an abstract concept because "it is important."

Since the days of the *Iliad*, great tales have been driven by characters. Where they are is of far less significance.

This is why movie stars in Hollywood get paid such astronomical sums. Viewers follow the stars. Millions will come to a Julia Roberts movie because it has Julia Roberts, even if it's essentially the same movie over and over and over. The fact that it sometimes may seem that the producers forgot even to hire a writer has virtually no impact whatsoever.

For more than a decade, for example, the most popular show on the Travel Channel in the United States has been *No Reservations*, a travel show based around the writer Anthony Bourdain.

Each week, Bourdain goes somewhere else in the world to check out great chefs, great food, or great restaurants. But the show is about him. Where he goes is an abstraction. People who watch the show don't really care about the destination. They care about Bourdain. No one watching suddenly turns it off if he is in Tokyo instead of Madrid. They don't say, "Hey, I'm really into Madrid, but I hate Tokyo." The location is an abstraction.

The most widely watched TV show on the planet as of now is *House*. This medical show is about the adventures of Dr. Gregory House, loosely based, so I am told, on Sherlock Holmes.

Each week, the plot is basically the same. A patient comes down with a weird disease, and House solves the mystery. The show is about House and his team. What the specific disease is, no one cares. People who watch the show (and there are millions worldwide) don't suddenly tune out because this week it's encephalitis and not polio. They don't care. Like the locations for Anthony Bourdain, the disease is an abstraction. What is seminal is House. If House disappeared, so too would the viewers.

Knowing this as we move into the world of video and TV, we are going to focus on a character in every video.

This week, when you go out to your shooting locations, I want you to proceed as we have before. That is, I want you to take a 20-minute break before you start shooting and find those seven events.

But then I want you to take a few more minutes and cast your video. I want you to look around and find the "star" of your movie.

Who is the star?

The star is the most compelling person you can find in the room. This may not be the person who owns the company or manages it. It may not be the person who brought you into the project. It even may not be the most "obvious" person. This will take a bit of "feeling out" the room. Again, it depends on your instincts.

The "star" of your video or film is the person you are going to bring home to your husband or wife and say, "Honey, guess who I brought home?" If the person you brought home turns out to be the incredibly boring head of the New Jersey Sewer Authority, Parsippany Division, well no amount of "but what he's saying is really important" is going to rescue you.

Your husband or wife is going to drag you into the kitchen and say, "I am sick and tired of you bringing home these losers!"

When you make someone the centerpiece of your video, you are essentially bringing that person into the viewer's home. Make sure that you bring someone interesting because if you don't, the next time the viewer sees you approaching, he or she will bar the door and turn out the lights. There are no second chances in this business.

The "star" of the video can be someone you saw on the location, or it could be you—if you believe that you have the drive and the ego to pull it off. That's your call.

Once you have cast your film, you are going to shoot it around and through the perspective of your star. This is going to make shooting and producing a compelling video much easier, and it's also going to make it much easier to watch.

Okay.

How do you shoot a person?

Until now, we have been filming what are more or less static situations—cutting the carrots, cutting the diamond, or transplanting a heart. All these "events" take place with a person doing the action being fairly static.

Fortunately for you, in America, people are static about 90 percent of the time. However, for that other 10 percent of the time when they do move, you have to know how to shoot them.

And how do you do that?

Here's the first rule: *Don't move the camera.*

Just like the static shooting—with one small exception.

Let's take a look at another hypothetical shooting situation.

Jane Jones is a concert pianist. You could just shoot her at the piano, but it's more interesting to follow her around a bit. So you meet her at home, where she is serving breakfast to her three children before heading off to a day at the studio. You are going to follow her.

You already know how to shoot her making breakfast. Close-up of the hands, close-up of the face, and so on.

And you already know how to shoot the kids eating breakfast. Likewise.

Now, she's getting ready to leave.

Shooting video is like playing a racquet sport. The more you can anticipate where the next shot is going to be and get there first, the more control you are going to have over your game.

Okay. Now Jane is about to leave the house. Everyone leaves his or her home in exactly the same way. What do they do?

They open the door.

Every single person leaves their house by opening the door.

And how do they open the door?

They reach out and turn the knob.

You know this is going to happen. You know what Jane is going to do. So now you can get ahead of the game and, anticipating the shot, set yourself up for an easy win.

So, if you know that Jane is going to go over and open the door, where do you want to be?

You want the camera pointed at the doorknob before Jane gets there. We call this *shoot where it's not.*

Now, hit the "Record" button and hold...hold...hold. And here comes Jane's hand. It slides into frame and turns the knob. Perfect. This says, "Someone is opening a door." Now, if the first shot is Jane's hand on the knob, or a close-up of the hand, what's the second shot?

A close-up of the face.

And the third? A wide shot.

Now, here is where things get a bit different.

As Jane starts to leave the house and go out the door, don't move the camera. Let her leave the frame.

Hold...hold...hold...until she is gone.

Now, run down the path to her house and get ahead of her by a good 20 feet or so. Then plant yourself directly in her path, blocking her. Get a nice clean shot of her walking toward you. Don't move. And don't worry. Unless she's a complete idiot, she won't walk into you. She'll walk past you. Let her leave the frame.

Now spin around and get a shot of her walking toward her car. Let her leave the frame.

Now (I told you this was like a racquet sport), run past her to her car.

Question: Which car is her car?

Answer: The blue Ford.

Question: How do you know that's her car?

Answer: Because you asked her when you were all having breakfast. You said, "How do you get to work?"

And she said, "I drive."

And you said, "Where's your car?"

And she said, "It's that blue Ford out there on the street."

So now run to the Ford.

Okay. Everyone gets into a car the same way. What do they do? They open the door.

And what does it look like when you open a car door?

You put your hand on the handle and open it.

So, where do you want to be shooting? A close-up of the hand on the door handle.

Which leads us to...a close-up of the face.

Which leads us to...a wide shot.

Hold, and let Jane get in the car, leaving the frame.

Okay.

Get in the car with her.

Now, everyone starts a car the same way. What do they do?

Right. So close-up of the hands on the keys. Which leads to...a face shot. Which leads to...a wide shot.

Sound familiar?

Okay. Now, because of the immutable laws of physics, Jane is not going to be able to drive out of the frame. She's going to take you along with her. So now point the camera out the window and get that shot you have seen a thousand times of the highway rushing up at you as Jane drives.

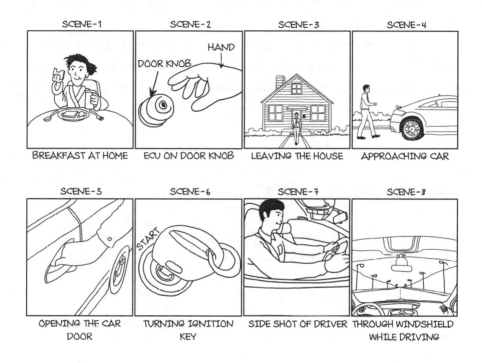

| SCENE-1 | SCENE-2 | SCENE-3 | SCENE-4 |
| BREAKFAST AT HOME | ECU ON DOOR KNOB | LEAVING THE HOUSE | APPROACHING CAR |

| SCENE-5 | SCENE-6 | SCENE-7 | SCENE-8 |
| OPENING THE CAR DOOR | TURNING IGNITION KEY | SIDE SHOT OF DRIVER | THROUGH WINDSHIELD WHILE DRIVING |

Now, let's think about what we've done.

Lots of times in movies you might see a "documentary filmmaker" go walking down the street, generally backward, following someone, film running the whole time.

Looks great.

I mean it looks great if you are watching the "documentary film-maker"!

If you look at what he or she has shot, you will see one shot, eight-minutes long, and an uncuttable pile of crap.

What we have done with Jane is to have taken an eight-minute event in reality and broken it up into 40 separate segments. Now, when we get to the edit, we can "accordion" the sequence. That is, we can make the event of Jane's getting up from the table and driving to work as long or as short as we like. Jane can get up from the table, walk out the door, and disappear. Or Jane can get up from the table, walk out of the door, and get in the car. Or Jane can get up from the table, walk down the path, ... and so on.

In the beginning, it may seem counterintuitive, but the *less* you move the camera when you are shooting, the more movement you get in the film. The *more* you move the camera while you are shooting, the less movement there is in the film.

So *don't move the camera*!

■■■Leaving So Soon?

The impact of not moving the camera while people are moving is that inevitably they will leave the frame. That is, they will "walk out" of the picture. Good!

You want them to do that!

Many people feel compelled to chase people around the room with a video camera. Don't!

Let them leave.

Why?

It's subconscious but very powerful.

If you are a viewer and you see someone leave the frame, you naturally ask, "Where did that person go?" This requires a resolution. So, in the next shot, either the person reappears or we cut to something else.

In either case, it continually drives the story forward visually. The viewer keeps asking, "What now? What now?" The more times someone leaves the frame, the better! The worst thing you can do is to chase people around the room with your camera to make sure that they never leave. I call this, "the subject who overstays his or her welcome." Keep leaving! Separation makes the heart grow fonder.

■■■ Objects in Motion

Shooting video makes you much more observant. If you shoot video long enough, you'll start to notice some basic traits about people. One of them is that, for the most part, people are pretty static. They don't move around a lot. Objectively, since we already spend five hours a day watching TV, that's already a lot of sitting. Add in working at a computer, eating, and sleeping, and you pretty much have it.

In the TV show *Big Brother*, the characters don't allow a TV in the house. That's because, all that the people in the *Big Brother* house would do, would be to sit and watch TV. This is inherently boring—unless you can watch the show that they are watching. If you look at any of the "reality" shows where they go into "regular people's homes," there's never a TV set around. On *The Bachelor*, there is never a TV set either. "Hey, I've got an idea. Why don't we go over to my house and watch TV?" Ummm...nope!

So, if you watch movies or TV shows, you would think that people are moving around all the time. There's a reason for that. Watching people move is inherently more interesting than watching them sit.

Remember the TV series *Miami Vice*?

Detectives Crockett and Tubbs were always jumping into a Ferrari or climbing into a cigarette speedboat and taking off across Biscayne Bay from downtown Miami to Miami Beach.

Once they jumped in the boat and started the engines. a Phil Collins song would start. Then there would be about three minutes and fifty seconds (3:50) of Phil Collins' music with lots of shots of them driving the boat, of the boat from a helicopter as it roared up the Inland Waterway, long shots of the boat, over the shoulder shots as they drove the boat, close-ups of their hands as they steered the boat, and so on. As the song came to an end, they would be pulling up in Miami Beach.

Now, it's actually a little less than three-quarters of a mile from downtown Miami to Miami Beach. A cigarette boat travels at about 40 mph. So in the length of a Phil Collins song, not only would they have plowed into the dock, but they also would have made it clear across Miami Beach and been somewhere in the Atlantic.

Clearly, the ride across the bay is not just to get there. It's to show that they are "going somewhere."

Think of the movie *Mission Impossible*. What do you see in your mind's eye? Tom Cruise on a motorcycle, going somewhere. James Bond in a car driving somewhere. It's endless once you start to think about it.

You can see the same thing in *Law and Order*. The cops are always jumping in the car, going somewhere. The lawyers are always "walking fast somewhere" when they're not driving.

Most lawyers spend their time hunched over a desk. It's not very interesting.

So learn from the best.

Movement.

The more movement you can put into your films and videos, the more viewers feel like they are "going somewhere"—like the film is "going somewhere."

■■■ Starting to Move the Camera

Okay. After three weeks of constantly pounding into you *do not move the camera*, this is an area that I enter with enormous trepidation. The basic rule still applies: *Do not move the camera*.

However.

There are a few situations where you may want to move the camera while you are recording.

But just a few!

This is not a license to start running around like a crazy person with the camera in record.

From time to time (and very rarely!), you may want to move the camera in record to replace an edit. That is, you may want to use the camera to move the viewer, editorially, from one shot to the next. This is called a *motivated pan*. That is, the editorial drive of the story (and your natural instincts!) will tell you when to move the camera. You move it in exactly the same way and at the same speed as you move your eye.

The more the shooting and editing can replicate how a normal person sees the world, the more the viewer will be drawn into the video you have made. That's the objective—to draw in the viewer.

How do you do that?

First, let's see how you perceive the world without a camera. Like everything else in this book, this is something you already know how to do. (You just don't know that you know how to do it.)

You remember the story about my students at Columbia University and how they used to shoot endless pans?

Here's a good experiment for you to do. Go up to 125th Street (or anywhere that is relatively new to you), and observe how you observe the scene. That is, how do you "see" the world?

You probably don't start on the left and slowly pan your head around to the right. More likely, you take in the whole scene. Then details start to attract your attention. A car comes down the street. A woman with a baby carriage walks by. You see an interesting face. A man yells, and you look over. A beautiful woman walks by. You get the idea. Still after still after still. This is how you see the world. In your brain, you lace these stills together to form a coherent narrative. This is what you need to do in film and video.

No one in his or her right mind walks down the street bobbing his or her head from left to right (unless the person has severe neurologic issues). But next time you are out, watch people with video cameras. Crazy! And unwatchable!

Now, I said that there are a few times (very few) when you can, in fact, move the camera while you are shooting.

When are they?

Let's go back to our first experience in shooting video: cutting the carrots.

As you'll recall, instinct took us to our first shot: a close-up of the hands cutting the carrots. Then instinct took us to our second shot: a close-up of the face, to resolve just who was cutting those carrots.

We followed the close-up of the hands with a close-up of the face because that is where our instincts naturally lead us. Seeing hands chopping carrots, we ask ourselves, "Whose hands are those?" and thus follow, both in shooting and later in editing, with a close-up of the face. One follows the other naturally.

In this case, we might want to move the camera, while recording, from the hands to the face. This is called a *motivated pan*. You move the camera exactly as you move your own eye, from one to the other. And you make the move with the same speed you move your own eye without a camera. Once again, you already know how to do this.

The motivated pan replaces an edit. This is not a convenience to allow you to wander around the room shooting at will and leaving the camera in record all the time. On the contrary, this is a very disciplined, very thought-out move that will appear on screen. Thus it must be as perfect as the rest of your shots.

Before you start the move, you must decide where the move is going to terminate. So plan that out first. Then, when you are ready to move, hold on the start point for a count of 10, make the move, and then stop. Hold on the end point for a count of 10. In other words, bookend the move with stills, at the beginning and at the end. Try this a few times. It's not so hard. You'll get the hang of it in no time.

You should have a minimal number of moves in any day's shooting. Perhaps four or five moves shot in an entire day of shooting would be a good target. Use them sparingly. Don't start moving the camera just for the sake of moving it. This looks amateurish.

■■■A Roadmap for Storytelling

If you were a builder, you would not start to build a house without a blueprint. You wouldn't gather together a pile of wood and nails and cement and say, "I'm sure there's a house in here somewhere." Yet this is often how most video and documentary makers start "creating" their vision.

Builders need a plan, a blueprint, and so do video makers and film-makers. So I am going to give you one.

If you follow this simple plan, it will deliver to you a perfect film every time. This is not the only way to construct a film, but it is one that works. Use it often enough, and in time, you will become confident enough to create your own approaches.

Today, we live in a world of increasingly short attention spans. And nowhere is this more evident than in the world of online video and TV. Inundated with content everywhere, we are married to an expectation of instant results, and we have no patience to wait for things to unfold. Offered a plethora of choices, the moment a viewer becomes bored, he or she is gone. Once bored by online video or a TV show, it is unlikely that the viewer is coming back to give you a second chance. Viewers have too many other options. And you can't post a sign on your website that says, "I know that was terrible last week, but I swear, I have gotten much better." Too late! Your viewers are gone forever.

If you watch online video, you will already be familiar with the habit of dragging the cursor along until you find something interesting. The key to success in online video or TV is to start with that interesting thing.

So each video, TV show, or film must start with the most exciting, most dynamic, most "Hey, this is amazing!" shot you can find. This is clearly something to think about when you are out shooting. What is that "killer shot" that no one can turn away from? Get it—and start with it.

This notion of "reaching out through the screen," grabbing the viewer by the throat from the very opening, and saying, "Hey, pay attention!" is not given solely to online video. John Ford, head of TLC, Discovery Channel, and National Geographic Channel, is a man who knows television. Once, at a meeting at the *New York Times*, he remarked that cable TV is "video flypaper." You have to "catch" people as they buzz by.

You catch them with a killer opening shot from the very first second.

Ever see a James Bond movie?

How does it open?

Bond is skiing down some Swiss mountain with people firing rocket-propelled grenades at him. A helicopter appears from nowhere, and he grabs onto it and is dragged into the sky. A missile goes off, and the helicopter blows up, and Bond drops back to earth and skis vertically down a rock-covered slope. All in the first 50 seconds.

Now, do you say to yourself, "I don't understand any of this. Who is chasing him? What's their motivation?"

No, you don't.

You just sit there and go, "Wow!"

Mission Impossible. Tom Cruise is riding on a motorcycle while he is being chased down some highway by three or four massive sixteen-wheelers all tossing explosives at him. Again, do you ask, "Why are they trying to kill him?" Not at all. You just sit there and go, "Wow!"

Lead with the most dynamic shots you have.

Take a look at *Lolita*, by Stanley Kubrick, a director's director. What is the opening shot of *Lolita*? Humbert Humbert is shooting at Quilty through the painting! Admittedly, *Lolita* does not have a lot of action scenes, this being the only one. And it's a scene that happens at the end of the film. But Kubrick has taken the most exciting action scene in a movie that is very much not an action film and jammed it up at the front so that the audience starts their viewing experience by going, "Wow!"

Remember the opening scene of *Fight Club*? The pistol in the mouth. Another action scene taken from the end of the film and jammed into the beginning, where it makes absolutely no narrative sense whatsoever but sure leaves you going, "Wow!"

Remember *Michael Clayton*? A great George Clooney movie. Remember the opening scene? A bunch of horses and a Mercedes blowing up. Actually, this is the last action scene in the film, once again jammed up to be the opening shot, where it makes absolutely no sense at all. But you sit in the theater for the first 30 seconds and say, "This is going to be good." The actual opening of the story? Lawyers at desks.

Remember the very successful TV series *ER*? The opening scene: An ambulance pulls into the hospital, lights flashing, people yelling.

The most watched TV series on the planet, *House*? The opening scene: An average person starts projectile vomiting in the middle of a speech, bleeding from the nose, having convulsions while teaching a class—you name it. Medical wow!

Law and Order? A kid hits a soccer ball in central park and comes across a young woman's body with a knife in her throat. Every single week.

So what am I telling you here? Learn from the best. Start with a "Wow!" shot or scene.

Okay. Now that you have the viewer's attention, at least for the next five seconds, where do you go?

I am going to answer this question by telling you a joke.

Ready?

■■■ A Pirate Walks into a Bar

A pirate walks into a bar. The bartender says, "Hey Pete, I haven't seen you in here for a long time. Where have you been?"

The pirate looks at the bartender and says, "I've been at sea for a year."

"Wow!" says the bartender, pausing to take Pete in. "That must have been some tough year. You didn't have the wooden leg when you were here last year. What happened?"

"Aye," says Pete. "Portuguese man-o-war in the West Indies. Cannonball tore off me leg. Had to get a peg."

"Wow!" says Pete, polishing a glass. "And what about that hook? You didn't have that hook last year. What happened there?"

"Aye," says the pirate, holding up his hook. "French frigate in the Far Tortugas. Shrapnel took off me hand. Had to get a hook."

"Whoa!" says the bartender, polishing the bar with a rag. "And what about that patch? You didn't have that patch last year."

"Aye, the patch," says Pete the pirate. "I was on the back of the ship and I looked up and a bird pooped in me eye."

The bartender stops cleaning for a moment. "A bird pooped in your eye?" he asks.

"Aye," says Pete. "First day with the hook."

Okay.

Do you get it?

First day with the hook.

He rubs his eye. . . .

Nevermind.

Okay. Here's the part that's important: What does the pirate look like?

Yes, I want you to take a moment now and describe to me what the pirate looks like—to you. What did you "see" in your mind's eye when you read the joke? What, for example, does the pirate look like?

What color hair does he have? Is it black or red? Is it long or short? Does he have a hat? Earrings? Is he wearing a vest? What color is it? Is he wearing a shirt? White? Black? Collars? Ruffled? Clean? Dirty? And what does the bar look like? What kind of floor does it have? Wood? Dark wood or light? Thick planks or thin? And the bar itself, what does that look like?

The funny thing here is that you can answer all these questions, and a lot more, with great precision. How many earrings? What color are the buttons on his vest? How many drinks are on the bar?

When I told you the joke, I didn't tell you any of that stuff. All I said was, "A pirate walks into a bar."

But that's enough. That's enough to let your mind set the entire scene so that you can understand the joke.

If I decided to tell you the joke without the narrative line "a pirate walks into a bar," you would have a very hard time even understanding the joke.

"Hey Pete, I haven't seen you in here for a long time. Where have you been?"

"I've been at sea for a year."

"Wow! That must have been some tough year. You didn't have the wooden leg when you were here last year. What happened?"

"Portuguese man-o-war in the West Indies. Cannonball tore off me leg. Had to get a peg."

"And what about that hook? You didn't have that hook last year."

You see how difficult it is to even understand what is going on here?

The line "a pirate walks into a bar" is essential to being able to appreciate and understand the joke.

Many bad documentary filmmakers and video makers have a strange belief that narration is somehow bad, that it is a sign of weakness. They believe that the best stories are the ones where you "let the characters tell their own story in their own words."

Nothing could be further from the truth.

The job of the pirate is to be a pirate. He is not a professional storyteller. You are. That is your job. Don't ask the pirate (or the musician or the painter or the sports figure or the suffering mother) to become a storyteller. They can't do it.

Sometimes filmmakers will spend hours or even days interviewing subjects and then dig into their interviews to lace together words or sentences that, when assembled, give a semblance of a narrative thread. This is not only a total waste of time, but it is also extremely tedious and difficult to do.

Let the pirate be a pirate. You be the storyteller.

You tell me the story.

If you were a writer for the *New York Times* and you went out to write a story for the newspaper about a pirate (for example), and you came back and submitted a story to your editor that was nothing but a string of quotes from the pirate, you would be fired on the spot, and for a good reason. Your story would be unreadable. Films and videos are no different. They need narration. And every story needs a line at the very beginning, the very first thing the viewer hears, that essentially explains what the story is going to be:

"A pirate walks into a bar."
"Fluffy the puppy was hit by a car and may die."

Get the concept?

Now let's go back to our very successful Hollywood movies and TV shows to see how this is already done. (You see? The process is all around you. It's not a secret. It's just that you have never seen it until now.)

Let's take the Bond movies. After Bond survives the attack on the Corniche in the south of France or the rockets on the ski slopes, he goes to M's office.

"James, a terrible thing has just happened," says Judy Dench. "A man named Auric Goldfinger is threatening to take over the world, and you have 48 hours to stop him." (This will happen as soon as they do a remake of *Goldfinger* with Daniel Craig.)

What has just happened here? The writers have said to the audience, in effect, "Okay stupid, here's the plot." This is the "pirate walks into a bar" moment.

Mission Impossible: Tom Cruise survives the attack on the motorcycle and gets the tape recorder. "An evil man has gotten hold of a nuclear weapon. You have to stop him. This tape will self-destruct in 10 seconds."

Same thing: "Okay stupid, here's the plot."

ER: An ambulance pulls into the emergency room. The orderlies go running through the place with the patient on a stretcher. An orderly from the ambulance says, "Twenty-three-year-old single mother with diabetes and gunshot wound to the head"—"Okay stupid, here's the plot."

Once you have gotten the complete attention of your viewers with your "Wow!" shot, you have about five seconds to explain to them what the film, video, movie, or whatever is about. This is the moment for your "a pirate walks into the bar" line. You have one chance here to address your viewers directly and say, "Okay, here's what this is all about." This is no time to get cute or subtle. Just be blunt. Get to the point.

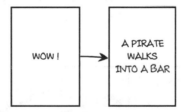

Now you've gotten the attention of your viewer—you have told him or her what this is going to be all about. Now is your moment to introduce your character, the "star" of your film.

As I said before, people like stories about people. They can relate to people. They have a very hard time relating to abstract concepts. So here is the moment to "introduce your main character." This is not an opening for a long, boring sound bite or an interview. It's just one line. Make me care about the star. The line should be limited to saying such things as, "I didn't think I would live to see the end of the day." And that's' it. Short and snappy. Stuff like that. Hold my attention, but don't start a lecture!

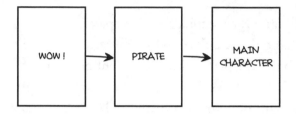

Okay.

Once you have introduced the star of your film, you have to give the viewer a reason to stay invested in the film.

This is called *the trip*. What is the trip that the character is going to go on? This does not have to be a physical trip (though that is the easiest: *Man vs. Wild*: Will he make it out of the jungle? *Casablanca*: Will Rick and Elsa leave Marrakech?). It can be an emotional trip (see Oprah's more than 235,000 iterations). It can be life or death: Will Fluffy survive?

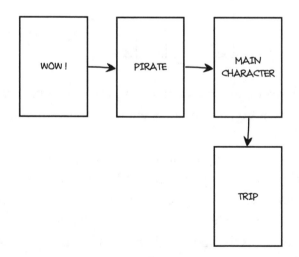

The trip sets us up for the *arc of story.*

The arc of story is the thing that answers the question, "Why should I invest the next minute of my life [next hour, next four hours, or more] in watching this thing you have made? You have to give me a reason to stick around."

Ever watch a countdown show such as *Top 100 Rock Songs of the 1980s?*

You know, the show starts with number 100 and goes backward to the number one rock song of the 1980s. Why do you watch it? To find out what the number one song was. And you watch it for all four hours! All four hours of commercial time.

If the show started with the host saying, "Okay, we're going to start with the number one song!" how long would you watch it? Maybe a minute to see what the number one song was? Probably. Any longer than that? Probably not.

It's the arc of story. The tension. The waiting to see "what happens" that keeps you there.

Ironically, all the other 99 songs don't mean a thing. No one sits at home and says, "Hold on here! 'Stairway to Heaven' is number 78! It should be number 67!" All the songs between 100 and 1 are, in a sense, filler.

Now, if you think holding your attention for four hours is a good trick, how about holding your attention for 13 weeks? Look at any of the elimination reality shows: *Survivor, The Great Race, America's Next Top Model, Project Runway*—the list goes on and on. What's the attraction here? To see who is the last person standing. The winner. The number one. The rest, as with "Stairway to Heaven," are merely abstract fillers. Nice, but in many ways immaterial.

If you think that this is not the case, take a show such as *Survivor,* and reverse the order. (It's all shot by the time you see it anyway.) Start the series by saying, "Bob here was the survivor. Let's see how he got there." Do you think that would rate? Me neither.

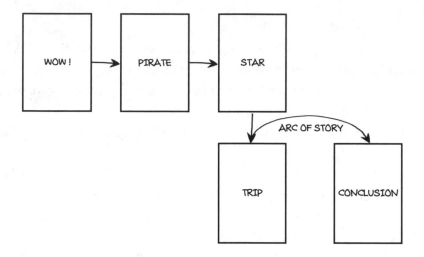

Here is an excellent blueprint for making a perfect and compelling story every time—whether it's a 1-minute video, a 90-minute feature film, or a 13-week reality show for cable. There are other ways of doing this, but if you start with this one, you will never go wrong.

■ ■ ■ Exercise

I want you to go out and gather up the elements for a very simple one-minute story. When you are done with basic shooting, I want you to sit down, have a cup of coffee, and draw a diagram like the one I drew above.

If you can fill in all the boxes, you are ready to come home. If you can't fill in all the boxes, shoot the parts that you are missing. Then come home and cut the film together.

■ ■ ■ ■ ■ ■ ■ ■ ■ ■ ■ ■ ■ ■ ■ ■ ■

10

Filing a Flight Plan

Assume that you get on a commercial airline and buckle in. The pilot taxis to the runway, guns the engines, and the plane goes screaming into the sky at 600 miles an hour. You unbuckle, wander up to the cockpit, and ask the pilot where you are going.

The pilot turns around to you and says, "No idea. But I'll figure it out along the way."

That would be unsettling.

No pilot flies a plane that way. They all file detailed flight plans of where they are going and how they are going to get there. They calculate such things as fuel consumption and estimated time of arrival (ETA).

It's amazing, however, the way that most TV producers and filmmakers operate. They fly without a flight plan. They grab a camera, show up at a location, and start shooting, hoping for the best. They want to see "what happens." They'll deal with it when it does.

This is a crazy way to work. From the very beginning, you have lost control of your work. You are perpetually playing catchup and forever at the mercy of chance. It's a very stressful way to work, and it makes for a very mediocre product unless you are very lucky.

Of course, unless you are shooting fiction, you can't script and plan everything, but you can file a "flight plan" for your shoot.

How does that work?

As with almost everything else in the video world, a great deal of what is going to happen is predictable; that is, you already know it. And, as with most of life, the more prepared you are, the better things will come out.

The secret to filing a "flight plan" for your shoot is to imagine the shooting day *before* it happens.

Let's say that you are going to shoot an event for a client's website. Let's say that the event is a performance at a local school. This is all pretty simple.

The night before the shoot, I want you to sit down and write out a list of all the elements you can imagine that take place at an event such as this. They might or they might not happen, but I want you to imagine everything you can think of. (This is not so different from the exercise we did with the restaurant a long time ago.) What are all the things that can happen at a school performance that you would want to shoot to make the "perfect" film or video of this event?

1. People arriving for the performance. They are outside the building, getting out of their cars, and going into the building.
2. Inside the auditorium, people are buying tickets, having their tickets taken, and talking. This is probably a good place to get a few sound bites about anticipation of a great show.
3. Backstage, the performers are putting on their makeup and their costumes.

4. Up above the stage, the technicians are getting the lighting and sound ready.
5. Back in the auditorium, people are starting to take their seats.
6. The lights go down, and the performance begins. You have a camera on a tripod shooting the performance.
7. You will need cutaway shots of the audience watching the performance, applauding, or sleeping.
8. The performance is over, curtain call.
9. People start to gather up their things and leave. This is a good place for a few sound bites. How did you like the show?
10. Backstage, the actors are exhausted, taking off their makeup. More good sound bites.
11. Outside, people are streaming out of the building, getting in their cars, and driving away.
12. The cleanup crew is sweeping the floor. The actors are turning out the lights.

Okay.

Is this a lot of stuff? You bet. And you haven't even gotten to the performance yet. But now, at least, you have a flight plan—a blueprint for the story that you want to shoot.

If you just show up with the camera, turn it on, and "hope for the best," you are going to miss a lot of stuff.

Now, let's go back to our flight plan.

If you actually shot each of those "elements," would you have a powerful piece? You bet you would. And if you shot each of those elements really well, how much time would each of the elements take up in your final film? Maybe a minute? Maybe 30 seconds? That's about right.

So, if you had two hours for the entire shoot, but you went out in a very focused way and said, "I have to get about three minutes of each of these things," that would not have been so hard, and you would have a great video.

On the other hand, if you arrived with no plan, spent the same two hours, but ended up shooting mostly the performance (which is what most people do), you would have a terrible piece.

Success is all about discipline and planning. It's about taking control of the shoot, as opposed to having the shoot take control of you and spending all your time chasing about playing catchup.

So, from now on, for every shoot you are on, whether it's a wedding or a civil war in Africa, I want you to file a flight plan the night before you "take off."

This whole notion of planning and discipline is intrinsic to success in this business. The better you plan, the more focused you are, the more organized and disciplined you are in your execution, and the more successful you are going to be in the business.

It's a bit tragic because for most of its history, filmmaking has attracted people who have none of these traits. In fact, they tended to skew to the opposite extreme. The vast majority of "filmmakers" today are a mess. Sloppy. Unfocused. Unorganized. Disasters. This is no bad thing for you. It makes the field even less competitive than it already is. But don't fall into that romantic trap of thinking that filmmaking is running around the world with a camera hoping to catch what happens. It isn't. If you can get organized and stay focused, though, you're all that much closer to success.

■■■ Imagining Perfection

Right on the heels of filing a flight plan, there is another mind exercise I want you to do the night before you go out on a shoot. I want you to turn out all the lights, lie down on your bed, and close your eyes.

Now I want you to imagine the best possible film that you could make on the subject you are going to tackle tomorrow.

For the purposes of this exercise, the shoot you are about to go on went great—better than you could possibly have imagined. Everything hit better than expected.

Then you took all your raw footage, and you cut the most spectacular, most amazing video out of it. Your video was so amazing that you posted it on YouTube, and Steven Spielberg saw it. He was so impressed that he flew you out to LA and offered you a three-picture contract with DreamWorks—it was that good!

Get the idea?

Now, what did that video look like?

Imagine it.

In detail.

See it in your head.

Let's say that tomorrow you are going out to a skate park to shoot a three-minute promotional video for a local sporting goods shop's website.

Fine.

What does the final video look like? What does the Emmy Award–winning, "Steven Spielberg just offered me a job" video look like?

Frame by frame.

Shot by shot.

This is your fantasy, so go for broke.

What's the first shot? What is the first thing you see on the screen? Imagine it.

Maybe it's a really low shot, with the camera at the base of a metal banister, and some kid goes sliding down that banister at like 100 miles an hour, and "Bang!" goes right over the lens. Right over the lens!

Do you like that open?

Pretty good!

If you like it so much, how are you going to get it tomorrow? You're going to have to put the camera down at the base of a banister and make it happen. Make sure that it happens. Because if you don't make it happen, it isn't going to.

You are in charge. This is what I mean by "taking control of your film."

I want you to imagine the entire video (it's not that hard—it's only three minutes). Then I want you to imagine it again, only better. Then again, but even better than that.

I want you to be able to hold the whole three-minute video in your head—your fantasy video. Your fantasy perfect video.

Then I want you to get up, turn on the lights, and go and storyboard out the film you have just made in your head on a piece of paper. Go ahead. Draw little boxes, and fill them in. Tell me the movie you want to make. The best, most spectacular, most unbelievable video anyone has ever seen on skate boarding in the whole world.

Now, when you go out to shoot tomorrow, you may not be able to achieve what you have imagined, but you can get close. And every time you go out to shoot, you are going to engage in the same exercise so that you always have a goal of perfection to shoot for.

When I was in my early twenties, I went to Israel.

One night I got into a big argument with some guy from the Peace Corps who was in Israel on his R&R. The argument was about Palestinians.

"Your problem," he said to me, "is that you have never met a Palestinian in your life."

He had me there.

"You should go to Gaza," he told me.

The next morning, I headed off to the Israel Tourist Office in Tel Aviv.

"I want to go to Gaza," I told the woman behind the counter.

She looked horrified.

"No you don't," she said. "You want to go to work on a kibbutz."

I didn't. I wanted to go to Gaza. I started to argue with her, but she wouldn't hear of it. Finally she said, "You can't."

That was more than enough motivation. The next morning I was outside an Israeli cement factory in Ashkelon. The factory employed lots of Palestinian workers from Gaza. They commuted daily by taxis. I chatted them up, and they offered me a ride in their taxi to Gaza. I went.

Once in Gaza, I made my way to Gaza Beach Camp and ended up living with a Palestinian family for a month.

The guy from the Peace Corps had been right. I had never met a Palestinian, until then. Several years later, I bought a small camcorder, quit my job at CBS News, got on a plane, and went back to Gaza. I moved in with a family in the Jabalya Refugee Camp and lived with them for a month.

I shot video every day. No cameraman, no soundman, no reporter. Just me, the camera, and the family. I wanted to see if it was possible to make video and television the way a photojournalist would cover a story: alone, intimate, with great images.

After a month, I came back to the United States, and I took my pile of tapes to Les Crystal, who was the executive producer of the *MacNeil/Lehrer News Hour* on PBS, whom I had never met before.

The work I had done was different. Unlike conventional TV news, with the reporter doing stand-ups and a few shots here and there to cover the track, this was more like a marriage of photography and film. It was intimate. It was powerful. And because I had spent a month with the family and in Gaza, I had gotten great access and great trust.

That had taken time. My name, after all, is Rosenblum, and for the first two weeks, they also probably thought I belonged on a kibbutz. But slowly, over time, they began to trust me.

By the same token, over all that time, living in that small house in the refugee camp, I began to imagine in my own mind what my film would look like. I stopped just shooting everything I could find or that happened and instead began to become much more focused and disciplined.

Les Crystal bought two pieces from me for $50,000, which I thought was pretty good for one month's work.

For PBS, this was a bargain. It was a lot cheaper than flying a crew, a producer, and a correspondent to Gaza. No airfares, no hotels, no meals, no cars, no salaries.

It was also a pretty good deal for me.

For the next two years, I traveled around the world making TV in this way. By myself, using a small handheld camera. As long as I went to the more dangerous places in the world, places that reporters preferred not to go, I could sell the work.

I went to Cambodia when the Khmer Rouge still controlled half the country.

I went to Afghanistan.

I went to Uganda and spent a month finding the index case for aids in the Ssese Islands. For that one, Ted Koppel gave me my own half-hour on *Nightline*.

I was having a great time.

Then, one evening in New York, I met a lawyer named Michael Tannen, who introduced me to Jan Stenbeck, a Swedish industrialist who was building the first commercial television network in Scandinavia. He actually makes an appearance in *The Girl with the Dragon Tattoo*, but he was a very real person.

Stenbeck immediately understood the economics of what I was doing and its implications. By cutting out the cameraman, soundman, producer, and reporter, I had vastly reduced the cost and complications of making TV.

Sometimes there is a moment when your whole life changes. I know exactly when that moment was.

Stenbeck flew me to Stockholm and then turned to me and said, "Can you teach other people to do this?"

I thought about it for a minute, and then I told him what I have continued to tell people for the past 25 years: "Any idiot can do this."

And they can. As long as they follow all the rules. The more you deviate from the rules, the more difficult this will be for you. The more you adhere exactly to what I tell you to do, the easier this will be and the better the product.

Shortly after my meeting with Stenbeck, by the way, I came back to New York. At that time, I was living in a small walk-up apartment in Brooklyn. I never thought of myself as anything more than a guy who ran around with a video camera making stuff. But my life was about to change forever.

About a month after my conversation with Stenbeck, the phone rang in my Brooklyn apartment. It was Michael Tannen, the lawyer.

"Mister Stenbeck wants to form a company with you," he said.

"Uh huh."

"He'll capitalize it with a million dollars and give you 30 percent equity."

I stared at the phone for a long time.

"Well, are you interested?" Tannen asked.

I was.

11

Finding Your Clients

Now that you have the skills, you're ready to begin to build the kind of business that can make you millions.

"But how can I do this?" you're probably asking. "How can I compete against media companies or production companies that have been doing this for years? Who am I?"

Ever hear of J. K. Rowling?

In 2011, *Forbes Magazine* estimated her net worth at $1 billion.

But she wasn't always so rich.

In fact, she began in grinding poverty.

J. K. Rowling, the woman who wrote the *Harry Potter* series, was a single mother, 38 years old, unemployed, on welfare, with no university degree. She probably did not look like the best of bets for a successful writer. In fact, she didn't look much like a successful anything.

If we ran literature the way we run TV, J. K. Rowling would have awakened one morning at the age of 38 and said, "Gee. I feel like writing a book. Harry Potter,...Harry Schlotter,...something like that. See, I have this idea....It's about a kid with glasses who..."

J. K. Rowling is talking about this "idea" she has for a book to a few friends, and one of them happens to know someone in the Human Resources Department at Random House, a big book publishing company. Maybe that someone will talk to J. K. about this idea she has. Who knows?

So J. K. Rowling goes down to Random House because they are a book publisher and that is where books are made. So, if you want to write a book, you have to get a job there, right? So J. K. Rowling gets her job interview.

"Okay, J. K., if that's your name. Slow down. You want to write a book, right?"

"Right."

"And you've got this idea, right?"

"Right"

"You know, J. K., ideas are a dime a dozen. We get lots of people coming here with ideas all the time."

"I'm sure, but this is a really good idea."

"I'm sure. Okay, J. K.—that's your name, right? J. K.? Funny name. Had a guy who applied for a job when I was just getting started. Called himself J. D. He didn't pass the typing test. Just as well, kind of a recluse. He wouldn't have fit in here at Random House."

"About my book?"

"Oh yeah. Well, look J. K., I have to be honest with you. First of all, you don't just come into a place like Random House and start writing books first off. I know that's what a lot of people think we do here, but it's not so easy."

"It's not?"

"Heck no. I know that lots of people see our books and dream about being Katie Couric or Oprah or one of our other famous authors, but believe me, there just aren't that many famous author jobs around. And it takes years."

"It does?"

"Sure. I mean, you just can't come in here and write a book."

"I can't?"

"No. And I have to be honest with you J. K. Your résumé is a little thin. I mean, for the kind of people we employ at Random House. You just don't look like 'writer' material to us."

"What do you mean?"

"Well, for starters, you're a single mother, on welfare. You're 38 years old. You've never written anything before. You have no university degree, and you have no background in writing or writing experience at all."

"So?"

"Well, we have people here who have studied writing at the graduate level. People who have worked for some of the best writers in the country, and they are still waiting for their chance to write."

"So you're saying..."

"Look. I'm going to give you a break. A real break. Probably the biggest break you have ever had in your life. And I'll probably get fired for doing it. I'm going to give you a job here at Random House......as a receptionist."

"A receptionist?"

"Sure. That's how everyone starts in the writing business. Even me. Paying your dues. You'll answer the phone, make coffee, photocopy things..."

"But I want to write."

"You'll get your chance. In a few years, if you do a good job, you'll get promoted to researcher. Then, if you're good at that, assistant writer, then associate writer; then, if you get really lucky, maybe...writer."

"In which case..."

"In which case you'll get to help our 'famous' writers to write their books."

"But what about Harry Potter?"

"Hey. Look. I'm sure this Harry Potter thing is a great idea, but we don't just make books off the tops of our heads. We do market research. Audience testing. Focus groups. But don't worry. After you've worked here for a while, you'll learn the ropes. Harry Potter…That's pretty funny."

Well, of course, J. K. Rowling starts as the receptionist, but after only a few years, she quits or gets fired in a corporate shake-up, and *Harry Potter* never gets written. However, Random House does publish that year, the 112th edition of its very famous series, *Writing with the Stars*. It's been a real best-seller since it first came out.

Fortunately for all of us, the world of books does not work the way the world of TV works. What has made literature so incredibly powerful is that it is open to anyone and that we take the time to teach everyone how to read and write. Now television, film, and video are open to anyone, and you are learning how to "write" in its language.

But once you have learned how to "write," and you have something to say, how do you get your work published? How do you start to make money out of it?

It's all about the content.

For most of the history of television, it was so complicated that just knowing how to push the buttons was enough to get you a job. Today, if you are going to succeed in this new world, you are going to live and die based on the content. If the content is great—if you can sit down at a laptop and do with your iPhone what J. K. Rowling did with her typewriter, that is, make something great—then you will be as big a success as she was. The major media companies and the world are always starving for great content.

So the key to success here is making things, but they have to be perfect.

■ ■ ■ Time to Start Making Money

■ ■ You Are the Production Company

When you think about owning a "production company," you are probably thinking about big offices in Hollywood or New York with lots of staff running around, glass doors, and your name on the wall. Not anymore!

You already own a production company with your iPhone. That's all it takes. Today, you have as much firepower as Disney or Dream-Works when it comes to putting stuff on the screen, and it's a whole lot less expensive to maintain. You can now do with your iPhone what J. K. Rowling did with her typewriter—create something great.

Your greatest leverage over places such as Disney or DreamWorks is that you have something they don't have: *freedom to fail.*

What does this mean? It means that it doesn't cost you anything to try. If it doesn't work out, you can try again and again until it does. This is, after all, how novels are written. The paper is cheap. If the first few pages don't work out, tear them up and start again.

Studios don't work like this, and they don't think like this.

Think of it this way. Suppose that every sheet of paper cost $1,000. When people put a sheet of paper into a typewriter (admittedly this is a bit archaic), they would type very, very carefully. They would be sure not to make any mistakes that would cause them to have to start again. And if every sheet of paper cost $1,000, every novel would start exactly the same way: "It was a dark and stormy night. . . ."

They would all start that way because every writer would be terrified of making a mistake and blowing the $1,000 that the paper cost.

But that's how TV shows are made now, with $1,000 pieces of paper. And that's why they all look the same. Because they are the same. Because networks are terrified to take a risk—the cost of failure it too high.

They agonize and budget and have massive overheads and staffs. You don't. You can try anything as often as you like. Just pick up the camera and start to shoot. In the end, you are in the far better position. In the end, you are going to win.

At the end of the day, after all is said and done, all that really matters is what's on the screen. As long as you can deliver a great product, no one will care how it was made, what camera you used, or how many directors or associate producers you hired.

By now, you should have enough skills to create video content that is as good as almost anyone else's—and for a whole lot less money.

This gives you an enormous competitive advantage. There is a whole spectrum of potential clients in front of you who are going to buy your work.

This will take time. It will take practice on your part, but if you work on it, you will progressively get better and better. I would not suggest pitching to a cable channel right away, but I would suggest that you can start using your video skills to build your own business or to make money making videos for others right away.

In any relationship with a client, you are only going to get one shot. If you do a great job, the client will come back for more. If you mess it up because you got ahead of yourself, there are no second chances. So my rule of thumb here is *slow and steady*. Together we are going to start with the easiest and most accessible clients and climb the ladder of success.

▪▪▪ The Ladder of Success

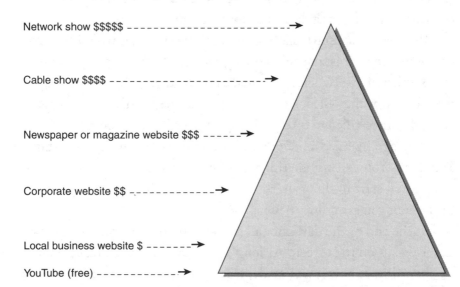

■ ■ Step 1: There's Plenty of Room at the Bottom: YouTube

No place is more evocative of the "video revolution" than YouTube. This site was invented in 2005 by three PayPal employees, yet today it carries more video than all the television and cable networks combined. As of 2012, YouTube had 56 billion videos, webcasting an astonishing 3 billion hours of video a month. By way of comparison, NBC broadcasts just over 700 hours of video a month. The contrast says it all, and we are only at the very beginning of this.

YouTube is also the second most heavily trafficked search engine in the world, after Google. More and more, if you want to find something, you go to YouTube.

Finally, by 2015, video will represent 90 percent of the total content of the web.

If you are starting in the video business, YouTube is a fantastic place to begin. YouTube is free. So are Vimeo, Facebook, and a whole lot of other sites that can show your video. Most likely, almost no one is going to make a fortune posting their videos on YouTube. There are a few exceptions, but you can use YouTube to sell your product or yourself, and even in that, there's a business.

YouTube gives you for free what networks used to have to sell—access to people's homes. Not so long ago, if you wanted to get your video message into someone's home, you needed to own a network or a cable company or hire a very expensive public relations (PR) company to get you on *The Today Show*.

YouTube changed all that.

Now, with YouTube, you can have your own "TV appearance" any time you want, all from the comfort of your living room.

Have you ever seen a product that touted itself by saying, "As seen on TV"? Well, now anyone and anything can be "on TV" all the time and for no cost. This is the power of YouTube.

More than anything else, YouTube is a great platform for sharing your work, your business, your product, or yourself. There are even a few people who are making YouTube pay directly.

Charlie Bit My Finger, the famous 56-second video posted by the Davies-Carr family, reportedly has netted them more than $150,000 in advertising appended to the video.

But this doesn't happen to everyone. Consider it "accidental" revenue.

YouTube says that it has more than 20,000 "partners" with whom it shares revenue from ad sales. It's interesting, but with more than 56 billion videos on YouTube, this is *not* a great way to earn a living with video.

A far better use of YouTube and video is for self-promotion and promotion of your business with a view to a larger end. Gary Vaynerchuk was a 16-year-old Russian immigrant working in his parents' tiny liquor store in New Jersey, Shoppers Discount Liquors, when he got the idea to start a video-driven wine information site on YouTube—The Wine Library. Setting up a video camera in his one-bedroom Brooklyn apartment, Vaynerchuk began to produce very simple videos explaining wines and interviewing "guests." It was like Letterman for wine.

Anyone can do this. Vaynerchuk leveraged off his "show" to build a $50 million business. His income didn't come from ad sales appended to his videos but rather from the traction that his regularly appearing videos gave him and his business.

Chris Kohatsu took one of our Travel Channel Academy (TCA) boot camps and then grabbed a video camera and started to post videos of herself online. She always had a passion for cooking and food and began shooting her own cooking videos.

Chris writes: "I knew there were so many stories to tell, people to meet, and experiences to share. My first videos were pretty poor in quality, but I stuck with it—I knew that video was a powerful communication tool, and I was determined to use it. It didn't take long for me to find my stride; before I knew it, my videos were being shared with others, distributed widely, and eventually bought!"

Chris eventually was hired by QVC to host her own show and by the Viking Range Corporation as an in-house chef.

Ryan Van Duzer had just returned from a stint with the Peace Corps and was uncertain as to what to do next. He knew that he had a passion for travel but didn't know how to make a living out of it. He also took one of our TCA courses, set up his own business, Duzertv. com, and began making and posting travel videos on his own.

In a very short time he began to acquire paying customers for his travel videos. These included CurrentTV, Lonely Planet, Out There Guy, and the Travel Channel. Now he has just gotten a full-time position as a host on *Paradise Hunter*.

Making videos of yourself is a great way to make that dream job into a reality. It's the "power of television." For a generation that grew up watching TV (the people who are doing the hiring), seeing someone actually doing something in video gives them a sense that this is "real." What you imagine, you can create. This is true whether you are Gary Vaynerchuk trying to reinvent a small business and turn it into a large one or Chris Kohatsu trying to invent her own career.

Michelle Phan is a 22-year-old YouTube phenomenon but also someone on the cutting edge of the vast potential that YouTube represents for those who are both motivated and talented. At the age of 18, Michelle's prospects did not look particularly good. Her parents were refugees from Vietnam who came to America with nothing. Her father abandoned the family when she was a child, leaving her and her mother to fend for themselves.

Michelle's mother had hoped that her daughter would go to medical school and become a doctor, but Michelle's interest gravitated toward art. She promised her deeply disappointed mother, "I will make this work."

And she did. She began posting how-to videos on YouTube about makeup techniques. She shot the videos herself, of herself—a kind of do-it-yourself *Vogue* magazine online, except without the *Vogue* part.

But the videos resonated. At present, Michelle has 1.5 million viewers. The Style Channel, by way of comparison, has 750,000 viewers.

If you were an advertiser, where would you rather be—on Michelle Phan's videos or on the Style Channel? In 2010, Michelle Phan was hired by Lancome. And think about the difference in terms of staffing, overhead, and cost of production between Michelle and the Style Channel. Who is more profitable?

YouTube as a platform is simple and cheap, and it clearly works. It is remarkable to me that more people are not doing this. People hire publicists and PR people to try and get them on local TV talk shows or radio shows in the hopes that this will build their business. The irony is that you don't need "their" local TV shows anymore—you can have your own, every day, and say whatever you want for as long as you like.

If you don't have your own liquor store or shoe store or restaurant or other business that you want to promote, you can create and produce the online "talk show" for those clients—for a fee. Not everyone knows how to create videos, and for the foreseeable future, there's a business for you if you can make videos for those who can't.

As demand for video skyrockets, and since very few people can create good video well, a window of opportunity has opened for those who are video-literate. It won't last forever, but you should jump on it while you can.

A similar window opened in the mid-1990s when the web suddenly came into play for businesses. Everyone understood that they needed a website, but very few people knew how to make one. Jeff Dachis and Greg Kanarick did, and in 1995, they were hired by the New York Botanical Garden to build a website for them. The garden project was paid for by Time Warner, who soon got to know Dachis and Kanarick and their fledgling company, Razorfish, which was run out of Dachis' apartment in Alphabet City.

Razorfish grew quickly, and by 1999, just four years later, the company had $260 million in annual revenues. This is what happens when you move quickly with new skills that everyone wants but few have.

Today, every business either has or needs a website. And every website needs video, whether the owners know it or not. If they know it, then you are the person to start providing that video for them. If they don't know it, then you are about to explain why video is so necessary to make their website attract more clients and improve sales.

Yaroslav Kaufman, another 22-year-old Russian immigrant, didn't have parents with a liquor store in New Jersey. All he had was a digital single-lens reflex (DSLR) video camera and a laptop, but that was enough.

He began to create promotional videos for clients, whatever clients he could find. Yaroslav writes:

At the time, I didn't realize that it would lead to the most unthinkable experiences and moments of sheer awe that have taken my breath away. I have traveled to parts of the world I would never sanely think to go. Namely, Deogarh, a remote village a day's travel from New Delhi in the heart of India. After filming a royal Rajput wedding, I strolled throughout the Mahal, past the elephant stables and through a labyrinth of corridors watching the sun come up and illuminate the desert plains. I helped my close friend start a video publication with which we have shot some of the best hotels, luxurious villas, and three Michelin star restaurants throughout the world. Cinema has put me into exotic automobiles, brand new yachts, and lavish suites in countries I only dared to dream of traveling to. My revelation was that learning this process is not merely shooting video, but it's rather learning a language anew, and one that is universally understood. This new communication tool has taken me from the shores of Sri Lanka to the Playboy mansion. I have been fortunate enough to live in places like historic Jewish Quarters in Prague, where I would go on morning walks, teach video workshops to journalists from war-torn countries, and listen to world-renowned mind readers share their secrets. What an incredibly gratifying experience it has been to live vicariously through my photography lens.

And the new world of video productions is not just limited to small companies. Kate Milliken got herself a video camera and a laptop, learned to shoot and cut on her own videos, and launched Milligrace, a Phoenix-based company that produces personal video documentaries. Says Kate:

I started Milligrace in 2004. We make "Videodes," video odes—high-end personal tribute videos for milestone occasions such as a birthday, anniversary, or retirement. We select and interview 15 to 20 people from someone's life, ranging from friends and family to first grade teachers. We then shoot about 6 hours of interview footage; create a 15-minute narrative; add old photos, archival footage, music, and graphics; and produce an emotionally packed mini-documentary. I have found through my work that if you make someone feel comfortable talking on camera about someone they love, they say incredibly articulate and beautiful things. The Videodes also level the playing field—a meaningful [sound] bite from a long-term housekeeper holds as much emotional content as a [sound] bite from an ex-president to our honorees because both have shared relevant personal experiences.

■ ■ STEP 3: CORPORATE CLIENTS

P. F. Bentley was a professional photojournalist for *Time Magazine* in the 1970s, but when digital photography became commonplace, companies such as Time cut their staff photographers, and the whole world of photojournalism came to a crashing halt.

Bentley was able to translate his photographic skills into shooting video, and today he lives on the Island of Molokai making promotional videos for clients such as Hilton Hotels for its online site and the Hawaii Department of Tourism, which suddenly discovered that it too needed online videos of Hawaii, and lots of them.

When I first met Francisco Aliwalas, he was living in a one-room walk-up in Hell's Kitchen. He had maxed out all his credit cards trying to make a feature film on his own, and it was not working out. But like Yaroslav, Bentley, and so many others, Francisco had a video camera and a laptop, and that was all it took.

His first client was an African safari company in Kenya that clearly needed a video. In exchange for a free trip to Kenya, Francisco delivered the video, and that was the beginning of a career in video production for online sites. Today, Francisco works with his wife, and they travel the world making videos. Francisco writes:

After working odd jobs, I used my savings to buy a Panasonic DVX100. This was the time when the world wide web was swelling with possibilities. Craigslist was my new manager, agent, and publicist. Thanks to the smaller, high-quality, affordable camcorders, Mac laptops, and Final Cut Pro, I'm a mobile television and movie studio. I've worked for clients such as NatGeo, MTV, Travel Channel, A&E, Nike, Coca-Cola, Camel, HGTV, Food Network, and CurrentTV. To date, I've made 15 music videos, a handful of commercials, documentaries, and more television shows than I can count.

These people are just the very beginning of what is going to be an enormous business—supplying videos to websites for just about every business there is.

The web makes it easy to find prospective targets for your new business. Get a list of the small businesses in your town or community or in areas in which you have an interest. Then check out their websites.

Most of them are going to be terrible. This is just how it is. But this is good. Most of them are going to need your help, and that is even better.

Make the first few videos for free.

What makes a good video for a local business?

Put the owner in the video!

People love to see themselves. A one-minute video about a local shoe store, clothing store, or pizzeria—how hard is that to do? Some graphics, some music, and...you're done. Make a video that features the owner of the small business. Make the owner the star of the video. Make the video short—30 seconds to a minute at most. The owner will love it. Let the owner post it on his or her website. It's an investment on your part. You're building a résumé.

The video also can be updated. If there's a sale. If there's something new on the menu. The link to the video also can be tied to a monthly (or weekly) mass e-mailing. There are lots of video-based services you can offer all the local merchants in your community.

Once you have done a dozen of these (and make them all great), you're going to be in a position to start charging for your services.

After all, if Joe the shoe store has a video on its website, Bill the competitor better have one as well! (Look at what a good investment your dozen free ones turned out to be.)

Now you can start charging.

How much do you charge?

The answer here is not a lot.

You want to build volume.

How much time does it take you to do one video? You should be able to crank them out pretty fast. So, if you're charging only a few hundred dollars, you're still in good shape. (And remember, this is the beginning of building a business, not the end.)

If you can begin to create a body of videos for your local merchants and make a few hundred dollars a week out of doing that, you're off to a good start. Those videos also can become ads for your local cable TV provider. By calling the cable provider, you can figure out what the rates are for a local ad buy. If the store starts to like you, you can begin to incorporate shooting, producing, and selling local TV ads as part of your production company business. The cable companies will like you, and in the not too distant future, you're going to start pitching them programming concepts anyway.

Another good target for your burgeoning video business is your local real estate brokerage. Real estate is a great target for video. It's online, it's entirely visual, and it has gone through a transition from text to photos. Now, no one can sell a house or rent an apartment without great photos. Video will be next. You can be there first. If you want to understand the power of real estate as a video topic, watch HGTV sometime.

Another great target is car dealers, both new and used. How simple would it be to start making 30-second spots about cars? (Just take a look at *Top Gear*.)

Finally, you can *create a whole new life for yourself.*

Hearing that I was writing this book, Tony Martin sent me the following:

My name is Tony Martin, and I'm from Washington, DC. I'm currently 32 years old, and I have traveled to over 170 countries as a travel filmmaker. Simply put, after flunking out of college, I floundered through life without a clue about what I wanted to do with myself, until I bought my first cheap camera.

If I had to describe my path in a few paragraphs, it would go something like this: In 2006 I met a man named Michael Rosenblum. He told me that the future of television was one man, one camera, one laptop. Not only was I inspired, I believed him. After landing a job on his television series,

5 Takes: Pacific Rim, *he taught me the basics of video journalism, which included how to tell a story with video, what shots to take, and the framework of editing with Final Cut Pro.*

Not only did I find a skill set, I found a passion. I took the foundation that Michael gave to me and built on it heavily through knowledge found on the Internet and practice. For the first time in my life, I had a purpose…I had something that I enjoyed and that I was good at. With a strong desire to chase a dream and a firm belief that you can learn anything on the Internet, I set out to become really good at making travel films.

To start, I took another piece of advice from Michael, "Just start making videos." One good video was all it took for the avalanche of opportunities that followed. In 2010, Coca-Cola wanted to send three people around the world, filming and blogging about what makes people from every culture happy. After a long interview process, I was one of those people selected for that epic journey, specifically for my ability to shoot, edit, and host videos all on my own. Although some countries weren't fit for travel, I sit here now with around 172 countries under my belt, amazed at all the places my camera has taken me. Just writing this makes me want to go out and shoot something. Actually, I think I will. ;)

12

Step 4 on the Ladder to Success: Newspapers, Magazines, and TV News

The world of newspapers and magazines is changing fast. The arrival of the Internet has completely changed the newspaper and magazine business. Those publications, which used to be the most stable of businesses, are on the ropes. They know that they must either migrate to the web or die.

And once they migrate to the web (and iPads and smart phones), they need video.

The problem is that they don't really have the vaguest idea of where to get it or how to produce it. They need you.

Welcome to the world of video journalism.

This does not have to be "news" per se (although it can be). People who write for *Vogue* are as much journalists as people who write for the *New York Times*. And both need video.

I have spent years working with journalism organizations all over the world, taking them into video. After I had spent two years with

Stenbeck building video journalism–driven TV stations for other people, I decided that I should own something myself. I went to some high-net-worth investors and raised a few million dollars. With that, I went and hired 100 or so National Public Radio radio stringers and former Time Life photographers, gave them video cameras, and taught them to shoot and cut their own video. I called the company *Video News International* (VNI), and within two years, I had more cameras and reporters worldwide than CNN.

In 1994, I sold a 51 percent interest in the company to the *New York Times* for $6 million, and overnight I became the president of New York Times Television.

I was not cut out for a corporate position, but I saw that as the web began to take off, newspapers and magazines were going to need video as much as any TV network. And because they had never been in the video business before, they represented a massive new opportunity for creating video content.

Every newspaper and every magazine is a great target client for you. As they migrate their content to the web, they need video, and they have no prior experience in making it. Some of them are trying to train their own in-house staff to shoot and cut their own video. (I have done a lot of these trainings myself.) The problem is that magazines and newspapers are already under enormous pressure to cut their staffs and their costs. The smaller staffs can barely produce the print content for the publications, let alone start making video.

Here's your opening. Solve their problem.

And it's not just websites. The arrival of iPads may have seemed the salvation of magazines and newspapers, but they are screens, and like all screens, they demand video—as do smart phones. More and more business for you.

When I went to the Columbia University School of Journalism, the school divided the class between broadcast and print journalism. Then print got divided between newspapers and magazines, and broadcast got divided between radio and television.

Well, guess what? Today, it's all video. Newspapers, magazines, radio, TV, and the web. All video, all the time.

And there are publications for every area of interest. Like fashion? How many fashion magazines are there? Sports? Home design? Boats? Tennis? It's endless. And all those magazines are going to need more and more video, all produced at a reasonable price point. It's a price point that conventional production companies and studios just can't touch—but you can, because all you need is your iPhone or camera and a laptop, and you're in business.

How do you approach these publications? Start sending e-mails. Get your sample reels together. Post them on your website and go. Just like that.

The great thing about news and the terrible thing about news is that when it's hot, it's hot—then five minutes later, it has almost no value. You won't see a lot of news reruns on TV. "Old news" is an oxymoron. It consumes content with a voracious appetite.

In the olden days, TV networks and newspapers had bureaus and correspondents all over the world. They're all pretty much closed down now, so even though the web and 24-hour cable have increased the need for content, the sources for that content have all but dried up.

This is where you come in.

The idea of being a foreign correspondent, running around the world with a video camera, is sexy as hell and fun. I did it for years. You'll never make millions, but if you're young and fit and seeking some adventure, you can have a fascinating few years.

In the 1950s, this was the life of photojournalists—they carried a Leica and went all over the world selling their work to publications such as *Life* or *Time*. Today, it's all video.

The trick here is to go someplace that will produce video that people are willing to pay for. This has less to do with where you go and more to do with the kind of video you are prepared to make and the clients you are selecting.

You are not going to be able to sell a lot of video stories from Paris to the *New York Times* (if Paris is what you are interested in), but I would bet that you could sell a few videos to magazines such as *Conde Nast Traveler* or *Gourmet Magazine*. Tailor the video to the client.

If you seek the thrill of wars and news, don't bother going to someplace like Afghanistan or Iraq. It's already far too competitive. The market is flooded with that stuff, and you aren't going to be able to offer anything too different from that which is already available for free.

No, if you want to break into the "I'm a foreign correspondent with a video camera" business and it's news, journalism, and interesting adventure you seek, then you have to pick someplace that is not on the cutting edge of news but rather on the margins but has potential.

Speaking a foreign language helps. China is a great target. Lots of interest, little coverage. India also. I spent years, off and on, crisscrossing Africa with a video camera. It's a fascinating place, but if you'll notice, you don't see a lot of Africa stories on TV news or in newspapers. If you could get into Iran or North Korea, that would be great, but be sure to go completely legally.

The trick here is to line up your potential clients, your strings, before you go. Make them aware that you are going, and don't hesitate to pitch them stories all the time. Post as much stuff as you can on your website. Something will hit.

Television is also a potential target client for you. After all, who uses video more than TV stations? And, if you can deliver a perfect product at a cost far below what it would cost them to send out a crew, a reporter, and a producer, you also are "solving their problem."

Initially, TV stations and cable news operations were reluctant to commission the work of "freelancers," preferring to use their own reporters and crews. But as the realities of the new world of digital economics begin to sink in, this will be less and less the case.

13

Week 6: The Big Money Is in Cable

This week we're going to go after the biggest fish in the sea—cable, where you can really make millions with relatively little effort.

Okay. Now we come to the big payoff.

Cable.

The future of video may be in webcasting and online, and in the not too distant future, you are going to see a convergence of broadcast, cable, and the web on your TV set so that you can't tell the difference. For the moment, though, your payday is still in the world of cable.

I have been running video training boot camps all over the world for years. They attract lots of different people. A few years ago, a guy came into one of my boot camps in New York, but he was no New Yorker. He had a bulldog neck, a clean-shaven head, wrap-around sunglasses, and a deep southern accent, and he was wearing a DEA sweatshirt.

Jay Russell.

Jay Russell had been a South Carolina state trooper. He was the kind of guy who would pull you over and say, "Boy, you're in a mess of trouble," and you would pee in your pants. He had run drug dogs—the kinds of dogs that can smell out drugs...and fear. A few years ago, Jay left his job as a state trooper and set up his own drug dog business. He would rent out his dogs to local law enforcement people or corporations to help them search for drugs or missing children.

When I met Jay, I thought, "There's a reality TV show in this."

When he finished my course, I told him to go home and make me a video of what his work was like.

He did.

We recut it several times. He got the help of his cousin in shooting and cutting it. We all met in New York, and after a lot of edits and re-edits, we had a two-minute video that I thought we could take around. We took it to Animal Planet, Discovery, and Spike TV and lots of other places. But at TruTV, we got a deal.

The people at TruTV wanted to go to a pilot. We partnered with Zoo Productions in Los Angeles, the same people who make *Are You Smarter than a Fifth Grader?*

The pilot was a hit—it rated, and we went into production on 13 episodes of *Southern Fried Sting*, starring Jay Russell, at $250,000 a half-hour. The series lasted three years.

Like so many other people, LaShan Browning was a producer at Oxygen Media when I first met her in 2000. She went through exactly the same training course that I have laid out for you here, from cutting the carrots to Fluffy the dog. But when LaShan finished, she realized that she didn't have to be an employee any longer.

Instead, she took her camera and laptop and founded her own production company, Red Moxie. In short order, she cut deals with Lifetime to do a series and then *Ride with Funkmaster Flex* for Spike TV, which ran for three seasons. Since then, she's produced and sold series for ESPN, WeTV, and lots more. She's her own boss and runs her own company, and she started the whole thing with a small camera and a laptop—and lots of "moxie."

LaShan's story is increasingly not unusual. Rather, it is the way all content for cable is going to be produced. There are thousands of cable channels in play. And each of those cable channels has one thing in common: They all need content, and lots of it. The big cable channels don't have much difficulty finding and paying for their content, but the smaller ones are in trouble.

If you own a cable channel, then you have to have content on it all the time. Otherwise, why own it? How is it ever going to turn a profit? So there are thousands of cable channels that want and need very high-quality, very low-cost content. That's your target.

For people who want to break into the cable business, I always say, "You have a machine in your living room that is giving you real-time, up-to-the-minute reports on what every cable channel is buying. Turn it on."

That machine, of course, is your TV. The cable channels already know what they want (for the most part). Just give them more of the same. Don't try to reinvent their programming. Just find another iteration of more of the same.

If you watch the cable channels, you will see that every cable channel finds its own niche and then does not deviate from it. Animal Planet does animals. The Travel Channel does travel, but mostly about food. HGTV does real estate. The list is endless. If you want to take a crack at the world of cable, give each company a variant on what it already has—just cheaper and better.

And if you are going to do this, pick a few channels that focus on something that you are personally interested in. If you get a hit (or even if you don't), you are going to have to live with this for a long time. So it should be something for which you have a passion. This will make it much easier all around.

■■■ How to Pitch Your Idea

People used to write up "treatments" of the video or show they wanted to make. Don't do this. Most TV network executives can't, won't, or don't read them. They spend their lives watching and making TV, so give them a pitch in video. Let them see what it looks like.

Once you have an idea for a show, you need to create a two- to three-minute pitch reel that sells the concept. Don't make more than two or three minutes. More is less.

You need to create something that is drop-dead perfect, even if it is only two minutes. Every frame has to be great. It has to jump off the screen. It has to be so good that when someone looks at it, they'll say, "I have to have that!" It has to start rocking from frame one and never stop.

Needless to say, a video of you standing in your kitchen making a chicken sandwich as a pitch to The Food Network is not going to fly.

If you're going to be successful at this, you have to make a very short video that never lets go. This is not a pilot. This is not a sample of the great series you want to make for Discovery or National Geographic. Instead, think of this as a movie trailer. It's a seduction. All great shots. Lots of music. The narrative should sell, sell, sell the concept.

What you want here is a reaction. You want the executive who sees this to pick up the phone, call you, and say, "You've got me interested. Let's meet." That's all you want, and believe me, that will be enough.

■■■ Don't Make a Pilot

One of the greatest mistakes people who want to break into this business make is that they create a complete pilot for the show they have in their head.

Don't do that!

Nothing will kill your chances at pitching a series faster than submitting a complete pilot.

This is a mistake people make all the time. A few years ago I met a man at a conference in Europe. He was trying to sell an hour-long documentary he had made about World War II. This was his personal passion, and he had financed the entire film on his own. No one wanted to buy it. He had been trying for years.

Now, it wasn't as if he didn't understand how to make videos. In his day job, he was a video producer for Playboy, but his real passion was the Second World War (go figure). No one wanted to buy his documentary because it was finished. The networks could have no input into it. Don't box the networks in. Instead, tempt them. Make them want to work with you, not buy something from you.

First, people who work in the TV business have very short attention spans—very short. Two minutes is about it.

Second, think about it. These people spend most of their lives in windowless cubicles. Their only pleasure in life is getting to be part of the production process. So that's what you want. You want them to participate in the production of your series. You want their input. You want them to fall in love with you.

If you give them a complete show, they are going to find 100 reasons not to like it. In fact, the more video you give them, the more stuff you give them not to like. As in all things in this business, less is more. The less you show (and what you show has to really rock), the more they will want more. The more you show at first, the lesser are the odds on ever hearing from them again.

■ ■ ■ What Kind of Show Should I Pitch?

Put yourself in the seat of a network executive. He or she just got the job as head of programming. Such people have a job life expectancy of about six months, just slightly longer than a fruit fly, and no wonder—they have a terrible job to fill.

When they come into work each day, they are confronted with a gigantic grid. Seven days a week, eight hours or more a day, often in half-hours, that have to be filled with programming. And that programming has to rate. It has to attract an audience and hold it, and it has to attract enough people that the ad salespeople can generate some income from it.

And they have a very small checkbook with which to fill those boxes.

And there are about 1,000 other networks with 1,000 other executives in exactly the same position, competing for the same viewers.

It's a terrible job.

The pressure is overwhelming.

And then, in you walk.

You have an idea. You love this. You have spent years and years working on this, and it's really important!

What's the idea?

An hour-long documentary on the coal miners of New Jersey.

Do you think anyone is going to have the vaguest interest in this?

I don't think so.

(Yes, I know, it's very important.)

But it doesn't fit the basic criteria of cable.

What are the criteria?

1. *The show has to be repeatable.* That is, it has to be the kind of thing that once you get the concept, it can be made endlessly. For example: *Deadliest Catch*—this is a show about Alaskan fishermen. You can keep this up for years. *Ice Road Truckers, Life in a Tattoo Parlor Anywhere in the United States, Real Housewives of Anywhere,* and so on. It's the concept that's endlessly repeatable. When you pitch it, you can envision it every week, week after week, year after year. That's not a one-hour documentary. That's a sellable concept.

2. *The show has to have shelf life.* That is, it has to be the kind of thing that you can show years from now. So it has no real-time events to date it. The networks like to run the rails off of these things, so you want to pick a topic that will be as interesting in 2020 as it is in 2012. This means that the story is more about what happens to the "characters" than specific facts and events.

3. *The show has to rate.* No matter how "important" the topic, no matter how well shot, no matter how good the music, if the show does not rate, it will not work. What rates? Things that have a "Wow!" factor. Things that make you and all your friends go, "Wow!" Here's a good test: If you've shot and edited a few minutes of your concept reel, show it to your own sample group. If they seem to be drifting, or if you have to say, "Wait, it gets better," it's time to go back to square one.

Okay, I've come up with a concept. What now?

Paper doesn't work. No one wants to see it.

What you need to do now is produce your killer one-minute concept reel. This thing has to just jump off the screen from the first shot to the end. Don't get hung up on interviews, long-winded explanations, facts, or anything else. Just go for the jugular. Test it with your friends or even people you meet on the street or in bars. This may make you annoying, but so what? This is your career we're talking about.

Once I would have said to burn 100 DVDs of your pitch reel and start sending them out. Today, that's a ridiculous idea. Instead, build yourself a website. Or rather, build a website for your production company. This is simple to do with WordPress, but it will give you a lot of instant credibility. Post your video on your company's website, along with lots of still photos of yourself at work. Also lots of stills of the projects you are pitching. The more stills, the better. Here's your chance to build yourself up. This is no place to be shy.

When I first met billionaire Jan Stenbeck, I was living in a walk-up in Brooklyn. He said to me, "You are the world expert in video journalism."

I had never thought of myself in that way—ever. "No I'm not," I told him, trying to be modest...and honest.

"From now on," he instructed me, "you are. Anyone asks you, that is what you tell them. Let other people say you're not."

It was great advice. There's a reason he became a billionaire.

Once you've got a pitch reel that really rocks and your website, you've got to get your video in front of a network executive.

Don't worry. They are as desperate to find you as you are to find them. Most network development executives have a job lifespan of about six months. They are always in search of the show that is going to save their job. It could be yours. It should be yours. But now you have to get their attention. How do you do that?

What you don't want and don't need, at least not at this stage, is an agent. At least not yet. An agent won't do you any good anyway, and no one can sell yourself better than you. But how do you get in front of the network?

Who these executives at the networks are is not a secret.

They publish their names at the end of every show they have something to do with. DVR the shows on your target cable channel that are close to what you are pitching. You want to get the names of the producers "for the network," not the producers for the production company that made the show. Big difference! The network producers will want to see you. The production companies will just steal your ideas!

Once you've got the name of the producer, it's time to do some online research. Google the producer. His or her life is no secret. Take a look at the other stuff that he or she has done. Then write the producer a letter. Be nice. Tell the producer what a great job he or she has done with *Real Plumbers* or whatever else he or she has produced in the past. How many people are telling the producer the same thing these days?

I like hard-copy letters. I find that in the world of e-mail and the web, mailed letters tend to get more attention paid to them. I also hand address them. Likewise, it tends to get noticed.

You can e-mail or write or both. I generally do both. What does it cost you?

The letters I write are short and very much right to the point. Why waste time? If the producer is interested, he or she is interested. If not, he or she is not.

In the letter I direct the producer to my website and the video I want to show him or her, but I always ask for a 10-minute meeting. There are few executives who don't have 10 minutes to spare for you. And if you can't get the producer's interest in 10 minutes (actually, if you can't get his or her interest in the first two minutes), an hour is not going to help. However, if you can get the producer's interest in those first two minutes, you're at the start of a much longer relationship.

If you get your 10 minutes, as in video, it's all about the open. If you can't sell yourself to the producer in the first two minutes, the other eight minutes are a waste of time.

No matter what the business, people generally invest in people.

If someone is going to buy your show, he or she is investing in you, not the idea. If the producer ultimately commits to 13 episodes, even at $100,000 an episode or $50,000 an episode, then he or she is writing a check for between half a million and a million dollars. That is still real money. It's an investment in the producer's future. If it fails, he or she will be out the door, looking for work.

You have those first two minutes to convince the producer that he or she can invest in you—that no matter what happens along the way, you are going to take care of it. You are going to make it work, you are going to deliver, you are a good investment and a good partner. Once the producer writes that check, his or her career is on the line along with yours. You are very much partners.

A few things will help in the meeting. First, dress well. Dress very well. Clothing makes a big difference. For better or worse, people are judged by how they dress. Dress for success. It's worth the investment. Filmmakers tend to dress like Michael Moore, if not worse. Don't do that. If Moore knew how to dress, he would be in Hollywood with massive studio budgets. He's talented, but he comes across as a mess. No one feels comfortable doing business with a mess, no matter how talented. Personally, I like Prada. It's incredibly expensive, but it immediately says, "I know what I am doing. I am a success. And if you work with me, you'll be a success too." For men, pay particular attention to the watch and shoes. Only the best. It's a good investment.

When you get the meeting, make eye contact—a lot. Be bold. Be certain. Be direct. Personally, I like to bang the table and say, "I will make this work." It helps.

Whether I am pitching shows or video content or a consulting idea or anything else, I try to write five letters a day, every day. I scour the local papers, magazines, and trades to find stories that show me an opening. The best kinds of openings are new hires. Mediabistro's Revolving Door, an online newsletter, is a great source of this kind of information. There's nothing like a new hire in a new job that wants to "shake things up."

These people want to make an impression with something new. You can provide them with that. They're good targets. Also, any news about new services, new platforms, new anything—any kind of change— represents good targets for you.

I have been writing letters like these for more than 20 years, and I have found that the ratio of responses remains pretty much the same. For every 100 letters I write, I get 10 responses. From each of those 10 responses, I can generally get one deal. This means that you have to be prepared for a 99 percent rejection rate, which is fine.

Having written five letters a day for 20 years, I have probably generated 30,000 letters. A 1 percent rate of return would be 300 deals over 20 years, which is about right and suits me just fine.

If your target is a cable broadcaster, the goal here is to get the exec to look at the video. You have to nudge him or her enough to take a look.

If he or she does take a look, the executive producer (EP) is going to have a very short attention span. This is why the video has to rock from the first frame onward. There's no room for slacking off here and no excuses. This is a very unforgiving business.

You want to create a video that makes the EP run down the hall and find his or her coworkers and say, "You have to look at this."

You can do this!

The EP's coworkers are no different from all those people you were annoying with your own man-on-the-street focus groups. How do you think big studios in Hollywood do it? You are no different from them now.

If the EP likes what he or she sees, he or she is going to get in touch with you. If the exec likes the video a lot, he or she is going to move from your video to a treatment—this would be more like a 5- to 10-minute video demo of what your idea for a show or series would look like. If you are good, you will be able to get the EP to put up $10,000 or so to cover the costs.

If you get to this point, put every dime on the screen. You can wait until later to take your just reward. Meanwhile, learn to love ramen noodles.

If the treatment resonates well with the EP's team, he or she will go for a pilot. This is a full-blown half-hour or hour.

The broadcaster will air the pilot, and if the pilot rates, you're into a series. The general first buy is 13 shows, but it could be less. At $250,000 per half-hour, you are now in business. Congratulations!

■ ■ ■ Don't Fall in Love

The secret to success here is volume. Don't fall in love with one show or one concept. You have to have 20 or 30 projects in play all the time. You never know which one is going to hit. Maybe none. Keep going. You only need one.

People who fail at this do so because they become fixated on selling their idea to a network.

You are not in the business of "selling an idea," you are in the business of solving a problem and selling yourself. This is, in fact, much easier and much more to the liking of the executives.

The executives have a problem that they have to solve in order to keep their jobs: How do they fill up that grid behind their desk with programming that will both rate and yet be so inexpensive to produce that the little they get from advertisers will make it profitable? This is a big problem for them.

Your job here is to help them.

Not to sell them your show. To sell them *you*. You will solve their problem. You can do it.

Do you see the difference?

So you have to be flexible.

"How can I help you?" is the approach you need to take. And you have to be willing to do anything you can to help them. They know their market. They know what their viewers like much better than you. If you can get their attention and they see a glimmer of something interesting in your one- or two-minute pitch reel, then put it in their hands. (What do you care?) If the network executives say, "We like this, but we think it would be better if it was based in Cleveland," your answer is, "Great idea!"

In fact, no matter what they suggest, your answer is always going to be, "Great idea!" Establish early the reputation that you are easy to work with.

I have been doing this for 25 years, and I always tell the people who work for me: "If the client wants tuna fish, give him or her tuna fish. Don't spend an hour explaining why the chicken salad is better."

Finally, if you get to the point of getting a network interested in your concept, the executives probably will want to pair you with an established production company your first time out. Not a problem; in fact, good news. But here you are going to need a lawyer. You don't want to become an employee of the production company but a partner. Go for it.

One last point: A lot of people always ask me, "If I pitch a show to a network, how do I know the network won't just steal it?"

This is a good question, but not one to worry about. There are a million ideas around, most of them basically the same. What networks are looking for is not so much new ideas as creative, talented, and driven people who can make content. That's you. And that's something you can't steal. Your videos are just your calling cards. The more you can make, the better.

14

Video: Your Path to Fame and Fortune

If you had told someone in 1452, the year that Gutenberg invented the printing press, that you now intended to make a living as a writer, he or she would have told you that you were out of your mind. As everyone knew, books were written by monks, and there were perhaps a thousand books in all of Europe. Plus, all the monk jobs were either taken or very hard to get. "Kid, this is no way to make a living," the person would have said.

Only 30 years after Gutenberg's invention, there were more than 15 million books in circulation in Europe, and suddenly, writing books was very much not only a way to earn a living but also a path to fame and fortune in a world that didn't have many paths.

If ever there was a quick way to fame and fortune in our own world, it has been through television. Nothing elevates people faster than a TV appearance, whether you are an aspiring comedian, a cook, a singer, a politician, or even a "real housewife." One day you're a nobody; the next day you're a "reality star," a "top chef," or a "clothing designer." And we're only at the very first days of the video revolution.

Once the ability to create and "broadcast" yourself becomes an everyday event, which it is becoming more and more every day, the door of opportunity opens ever wider for those willing to walk through it—and you don't have to wait to pass the auditions for *American Idol*. *Today, you are your own audition.*

The groundwork for our television-driven world was laid 50 years ago when Americans became addicted to TV viewing and we became a TV-based culture. Once television was introduced in the 1950s, TV sets became the fastest adopted appliance in history. That is, within about a decade, Americans went from never having watched TV to an almost insatiable desire for it. By the early 1960s, less than a decade after TV's introduction, there was a TV set in almost every home in America.

And the medium itself became all-pervasive, driving almost every activity from news and information, to sports, to what kind of music people bought and listened to, to what they ate, to their feelings about race, to who they elected for president.

Today, this has not changed. In fact, the habit has only accelerated. The arrival of the web, smart phones, and iPads only serves to increase TV watching as a habit, in the sense of TV as video on a screen. "TV Everywhere" is the mantra of every major broadcaster, so much so that in 2009, Time Warner and Comcast actually launched something called the *TVE Initiative*, for "TV Everywhere."

When Tim Berners Lee invented the World Wide Web in 1989, there was only a handful of TV networks in the world. All the content related to television came from a few executives in a handful of network offices in New York or Los Angeles. Those few executives decided what everyone else in America would watch and, in effect, know about a subject or even think about it. Thirty years later, there are more than

56 billion videos on YouTube, and every website has a video—and we are just getting started. This is the pure "democratization" of the most powerful medium in the world, and that is no bad thing.

But now, as the technology grows exponentially, video begins to transcend even the screens and enter into every aspect of day-to-day life, from "Pump TV" at gas stations to "Airport TV" to "Elevator TV."

And this is only going to continue to grow at an even faster rate.

This growth is driven by Moore's law, a law that has become as immutable as gravity when it comes to technology. The law is named for Gordon Moore, one of the founders of Intel. In 1965, Moore predicted that computer speed would double every two years, whereas the cost of the microprocessors would halve during the same time frame. This law has proven remarkably true since then, and it applies not just to computer processors but also to everything that is built on that technology—including video cameras and editing systems.

Here's an easy way to think about the incredible power of Moore's law: Take a chess board. Put a single grain of rice on the first square. Then double it on the second square. Double it again on the third square, and so on. What happens?

1	2	4	8	16

One becomes 2, which becomes 4, which becomes 8, which becomes 16, which becomes 32, which becomes 64, which becomes 128, which becomes 256, which becomes 512. Thus 1,...2,...4,... 8,...16,...32,...64,...128,....256,...512,...1044 (or 1K),...2K,... 4K,...8K,...16K,...32K,...64K,...128K,...256K,...512K,...and so on across the board.

1	2	4	8	16	32	64	128
256	512						
							2^{63}

By the time the sixty-fourth square is reached, or would have been reached, for no one could in fact ever get there, it would have taken 9,223,372,036,854,775,808 grains of rice. This is 9 quintillian or 9 billion billion grains of rice. That's a lot of rice.

Does the run of numbers look familiar to you? That is, 1, 2, 4, 8, 16, 32, 64, 128, 256, 512, and so on?

It will if you know anything about computers.

The run of numbers represents not only grains of rice but also the processing speeds of computer chips.

1	2	4	8	16	32	64	128
256 calculator 1967	512 1969	1044 1971	2k 1973	4k 1975	6k 1977	8k 1979	16k 1981
32k 1983	64k 1985	128k 1987	256k 1989	512k 1991	1044m 1993	2m 1995	4m 1997
8m 1999	16m 2001	32m 2003	64m 2005	128m 2007	256m 2009	512m 2011	

The ninth square is where we were in 1967, when computer chips were just barely fast enough to run a calculator. This was the era of Hewlett-Packard. Since each square represents two years, by 1973, you get the first Atari games and Nolan Bushnell. Jump ahead to 1977, and now processors are fast enough for Steve Jobs to launch the Apple II. Moore's law just keeps making the processors faster and cheaper. Soon computers could handle word processing, graphics, music, and even video. Faster and cheaper, faster and cheaper. And this is a trend that is going to continue.

This is the reason that mobile phones, which were once the size of bricks, are now not only pocket-sized but also are really tiny computers—and they are only going to get faster, better, smaller, more powerful, and cheaper. The same holds true for video cameras. Those giant things that professional camera operators once slung on their shoulders are now embedded in your iPhone and most likely, in another few years, will be embedded in your eye glasses and be even better.

What this means for you the video maker is that not only are the cost and complexity of producing professional quality video going to continue to drop, but the number of platforms that need produced video is going to expand exponentially.

Look around you and observe how much of your world is immersed in print—from signs on the sides of buses to newspapers to magazines to advertisements in stores. All of this, all of it, is going to be video in the next decade or so. These are your clients. This is your future. It is a future that is only beginning to come to life, but you are positioned to be on the very ground floor of a whole new world.

My wife and I recently bought a food processor. We consider ourselves to be fairly technically literate, but it turned out to be a rather complicated machine. When we couldn't figure out how to make breadcrumbs, I went searching for the owner's manual—something we make a religious habit of *not* reading for any appliance.

Instead of an owner's manual, Cuisinart enclosed a DVD with a video that explained how the machine worked—and how to make breadcrumbs. Beats reading!

Soon every product, every appliance, and almost every transaction is going to require an explanatory video. Short videos, simple and to the point.

Video cooking instructions and lessons. What to wear. How to dress. How to decorate your home. Home repair. Child care. Baby care. Home medical information. And that's just the beginning.

Howcast, an online instructional video site with videos teaching you such stuff as "How to kiss" and "How to get a great date," was launched just two years ago and is valued today at $20 million. You can do this too.

A few years ago, there was no "online dating," but there were classified ads: "Thirty-two-year-old single woman, blah blah blah." They were in text, and they were, well, in text. Then came online dating, and pretty soon there were photos. In fact, the photos became so much the driver of who got the dates and who didn't that businesses began to spring up producing professional head shots for online dating sites.

Soon those sites are going to go to video. It's inevitable.

And who is going to make the videos for those sites?

The same holds true for used-car sales, new-car sales, real estate sales, and inevitably, everything sold on eBay or anywhere else. They are all going to need video. Just as you would never post a classified ad to sell a house without photos (something that was common only a few years ago), in the near future no one will be able to post an ad for a house, a car, or a boat without video. And who is going to make those videos?

How about you?

■■■ A Word About Politics and Video

Eighty-five percent of Americans get most of their news and information from television. So what television news decides to cover shapes the way we see the world. But television coverage is expensive—at least when the networks make the content themselves. So there are lots of places that news won't go. And if television doesn't go there, that place or that story ceases to exist in the public mind.

Until now, the networks and cable news operations have had a monopoly on what got covered and what you got to see and know about. This has enormous ramifications.

Take a whole country such as Bangladesh. The only time CNN or the BBC will send a crew to Bangladesh is when there is a flood, a famine, or a disaster of some kind. Other than that, Bangladesh ceases to have any presence in the public mind.

What is the upshot of this?

If I say to you, "Bangladesh," close your eyes and tell me what you see. Famine? Flood? Starving children? Would you consider taking a vacation to Bangladesh? Would you consider opening a business in Bangladesh? I don't think so. The image has been corrupted by the kind of coverage the country gets.

But why should Bangladesh be at the mercy of the assignment desk at CNN? Does this make any sense? How much simpler for Bangladesh to take control of its own destiny and image and produce its own content and flood the blogosphere and cable world with that instead. And look at how simply that could be done.

Palestinians living in Gaza and the West Bank strap on explosives and walk into Israeli cafés and blow themselves up.

They aren't doing this to protest Israeli coffee. They are doing this in the hopes of attracting CNN or the BBC to come to the West Bank and report on how terrible their plight is. Time to cut out the middleman. How much simpler to equip Palestinians with video cameras and laptops and teach them to flood the world media marketplace with an endless stream of videos simply telling their own story. Perhaps they might even buy commercial time on Israeli TV to make their case.

One of my clients is the United Nations High Commissioner for Refugees (UNHCR). These people operate all over the world in some of the most horrific conditions imaginable. They were in Darfur years before the rest of the world even knew what Darfur was. The rest of the world learned about Darfur when CNN finally sent in a crew, but that took time, and millions suffered in the interim.

I've been equipping the UNHCR people with small cameras and laptops and teaching them to shoot and cut their own stories and post them online and flood the blogosphere. They don't have to wait for CNN to decide to arrive. CNN or the BBC certainly can air their stories—but if they don't, others will.

15

Quo Vadis?

In 2000, I opened a video café on the Lower East Side in Manhattan. It was called DV Dojo. It was across the street from CBGB on the Bowery.

The idea was pretty simple. It was going to be like an Internet café, but instead of having computers where people could send e-mails, I would have computers that would have Final Cut Pro on them.

I also bought a bunch of Canon GL2 cameras and ran classes on how to shoot and cut. I put in a massive projection system so that I could show people's finished films on Friday nights.

I thought it was a pretty cool idea. However, $700,000 and one divorce later, it probably was not as cool as I thought it was when I started, but it did have an interesting side effect.

One day, early in the history of DV DOJO (perhaps another reason why it failed), a big (very big) man named Jamie Daves came into the place. We started talking, and I gave him a coffee and a long discourse on the "video revolution," the democratization of television, and of course, Gutenberg.

A few days later I was in London when Jamie Daves called me.

"Do you remember me?" he asked.

I did.

"I represent former Vice President Al Gore," he told me, "and the vice president would like to meet with you."

Gore had only recently lost the 2000 election for the presidency. Why in the world he wanted to meet with me was totally beyond me.

"When are you going to be in New York?" Daves asked.

I was coming back in a few days, so we set a date.

"The vice president wants to know if there is some place private that you can meet."

"He can come to my house," I said. That was pretty private.

So a few days later I went back to New York.

In those days, I was living in a loft in Soho, still with Glenda, my soon-to-be ex-wife. When I got home, I told her Al Gore was coming to see me tomorrow. She stared at me with that look that says it's time to hire a divorce lawyer, and a good one. She rolled her eyes and said, "Yeah! Right! Al Gore!" and walked away.

The next morning at 8 a.m. my doorbell rang. I looked at the little video monitor that New York lofts have, and there, downstairs, was Al Gore. I buzzed him in. "Come on up!"

We sat down at my dining room table.

He was equipped with legal pads, pens, and a pocket protector.

"I have an idea for starting a new cable channel," Gore began. "There's a whole revolution going on in the world of video. It's a lot like Gutenberg. If you were born 500 years ago, you would have been a serf...."

I stared at him for a while. "You have no idea who you are talking to," I said, and it was off to Medieval Germany for an hour or so.

Just then, there was a disturbance in the kitchen.

Gore looked up.

"That's probably my wife," I said. "Just getting up." Glenda was not among the early risers. "Why don't you go in and say hello?"

Gore got up from the table and strode into the kitchen, his hand extended. "Hi! Al Gore!"

The expression on my soon-to-be ex-wife's face was worth all the long hours I would later spend in court, not to mention the legal fees.

Over time, we formed a cable channel called *CurrentTV*. The basis of CurrentTV was the "user-generated" revolution—that viewers would make their own content.

No one had ever done anything like this before, so it was an unknown. Once we started to get the word out, we could see what the response was.

Sometime later, Lisa (my new wife, thank God) and I were in the offices of CurrentTV in San Francisco when a mail truck backed in. This was in the days before you could even upload video to the web. The truck began unloading sacks of mail, all filled with DVDs and VHS tapes of the work people had done on their own. It was like the final scene from *Miracle on 34th Street*. Bag after bag after bag. We easily had 20,000 responses, and that was the first day. They just kept coming.

The experience with CurrentTV taught me two things right away:

1. Millions of people were dying to make their own content.
2. Ninety-nine percent of it was junk.

It was junk because no one had ever taught them how to make video.

A few months later I was in London when I heard that Pat Younge, an executive at BBC Sports, had just gotten hired to be the new head of the Travel Channel in the United States. Discovery Networks had a long history of swapping executives with the BBC.

"Congratulations and condolences," I told him.

"Why?" he asked.

The Travel Channel, despite its extremely interesting premise, had always been the dog among the Discovery group. God only knows why.

"I have an idea," I said to Pat. So he, Lisa, and I met in London.

"I learned two things from the CurrentTV experience," I told him. "Lots of people are making content, and no one knows what they are doing." We came up with the idea of an academy, run in partnership with the Travel Channel, where anyone could sign up and take one of our intensive four-day boot camps to learn to make travel videos and even Travel Channel TV shows. We would charge the participants $2,000 for the four-day experience.

Pat said that he wasn't sure if anyone would really sign up for this, so he said, "I'll run the ads, but if we don't get a dozen people to sign up, we'll kill it."

We all agreed.

Twenty-hour hours after the first ads ran, we had 500 people who wanted to take the course.

We had hit on something very interesting and very basic.

It turns out that in the world of Facebook and social networks, people no longer just want to be passive observers of TV. They want to make it as much as they want to watch it. This desire obviously culminates in, among other things, the 56 billion and counting videos posted to YouTube. The problem is that while people have a deep desire to make content, no one ever taught them exactly how to do it.

Thus the Travel Channel Academy (TCA) and later other academies all over the world. After a few years, we saw that for every 100 people who came to the website to sign up for TCA, only one did.

"Two-thousand dollars is a lot to charge," Lisa remarked. So she came up with the idea of translating all the in-person training to an online site called *New York Video School* (www.nyvs.com). It was a subscription site with more than 350 instructional videos covering every aspect of video production, sales, and so on.

We launched it in 2009, and two years later, we had more than 20,000 members, and it's just getting started.

In fact, by buying this book, you've also become a member. All you have to do is go to www.nyvs.com and enter the code D856EE859 for a free two-month initial membership. It covers in video a lot of what we have already covered in the book, but it also will give you a chance to shoot your own video and upload it and share it with other members.

Everyone on the site has already "cut the carrots" themselves.

Now you may be thinking, despite all you have read here, "Well, this is all very interesting, but I'm sure some big media companies are going to pick up the ball here. This is so obvious. What chance do I possibly have against them?"

You have every chance in the world because if history teaches us anything, it teaches us that big corporations can't change the way they think. But you can.

The day after I met with Ted Turner, I got on a plane and went down to Atlanta to see Pat Mitchell, as he had instructed. She was friendly when she came to greet me in the lobby. I had, after all, been sent by her boss, Ted Turner.

When we got into her office, though, her demeanor changed. She slammed the door and turned, lightning bolts coming out of her eyes.

"How did you get to him?" she demanded.

"I wrote him a letter," I said, pretty astonished at her instant hostility.

"Well, we know all about what you are doing, and we are not interested," she said.

And that was that.

I went back to Turner and told him. He said, "I can't make my people do what they don't want to do."

CNN did start iReport, a kind of "citizen journalist" service where "average people" were encouraged to pick up a home video camera and shoot news if they saw something happen. What CNN was looking for was what we might call "accidental video." That is, if a tornado happens to hit your house, shoot some video for us, and we'll put it on air, maybe.

CNN has an astonishing 750,000 iReporters registered on its website. It shows that people want to do this.

CNN could have 750,000 cameras reporting for it daily all over the world. But it doesn't. It could harness this vast power, but it doesn't.

CNN doesn't really want to open the door to this. In their hearts, CNN executives don't trust it. Like so many other companies from Kodak to NBC, CNN can only see the new technology through the way it has always worked—a reporter and a cameraman and a producer. And it is unlikely that CNN executives will ever be able to wrap their heads around the idea that someone besides their employees could ever make content.

That is your leverage.

That is your opening.

They won't be able to change. And they are not alone. I have presented this concept to every major broadcaster in the world. They all agree that it is "going to happen one day," but not today.

But today is very much the day for you. The fact that the technology and potential are there and broadcast executives refuse to move or move fast enough is all you need to succeed. Get your camera and get started. You have nothing to lose and everything to gain. But you won't make your millions by talking about it. You have to start making content.

In the beginning, your content will not be great. In fact, it probably will be terrible. Don't let that deter you! Keep at it. The more you do, the better you are going to get. Your great advantage over broadcasters is that it costs them millions to commission a pilot or a film. It costs you nothing to try to keep on trying until you get it right. And send it to me. I want to see it.

Your winning edge here is not just the far lower cost of making content, but it's also what the content is. Here is where you really have a chance to change the world and make your own mark. Your success here does not depend on how well you light a scene or how good your music track is. The key to success, in fact, is much easier than that. It's all about *authorship*.

Authorship is the thing that is lacking in television and videos, and it's a wide-open field, ready for you whose time is now.

Television and video are incredibly plastic media. They are about manipulating pictures, sound and music, and graphics and writing and stories. When we watch them, we should be astonished at how powerful they are. Instead, we are generally astonished at how banal and terrible they are. Cats stuck in trees, *Charlie Bit My Finger*, or *Cupcake Wars*. There's plenty of room at the top.

Consider this: If you wake up one morning and decide that you want to write a book, you get out your laptop, and you start writing. Maybe you write something great, and maybe you write junk. And if you start writing junk, you just delete and start again, and again, until you get it right. This is where great novels come from. They don't come from employees at Random House; they come from people sitting at home at their kitchen tables cranking out ideas from their own heads on their laptops in their own time.

If you wake up one morning and decide that you want to become a musician, you get yourself a guitar and head for the garage and start rocking out. Maybe you're great, and you're the next Sting, or maybe you're just the next "stink," but the only way to know is to try and maybe try again until you get it right or don't.

If you wake up one morning and decide that you want to be an artist, you get yourself a canvas and some paint, and you have a go at it. Maybe you're the next Picasso, maybe you're not, but the only way to find out is to try and keep trying.

Of all the creative media in the world, television is the only one that says, "If you wake up one morning and decide that you wanted to make TV shows, you get yourself a job at a production company or a network making coffee and phone calls."

This is why television and video have, until now, been so terrible. Five hundred channels and nothing to watch. There is a reason. No personal authorship. Everything is cookie-cutter.

If you went to the Metropolitan Museum of Art in Manhattan and you took all the paintings and piled them up on Fifth Avenue, you would have a stack that reached a few hundred feet high. Yet, in that stack, you would have Michelangelos, Rembrandts, and DaVincis and a whole lot more. These things represent the pinnacle of what we can do with the art of paint and canvas.

I have now been making video and TV for more than 60 years—24 hours a day, 365 days a year on hundreds, if not thousands of channels. This is a massive amount of content that already has been made. And if you took all the TV content that has ever been made and stacked it up in a pile, it probably would reach from here to the moon. Yet, if you combed through it, you would be hard-pressed to find what we could call the "Michelangelo of television"—the paragon, the best of what this medium can do.

There's a reason for this. Until now, television has been so expensive and complicated to produce that it has been done by corporations and committees. And corporations and committees don't produce brilliance. They produce *Cupcake Wars*.

The question, of course, is why? Why do we, despite the billions of dollars spent on TV and the billions of hours devoted to it, continue to produce garbage?

Because creativity requires a personal vision.

When Picasso woke up and got the vision for *Guernica*, he simply went up to the atelier and started to paint. This is how great paintings are made. This is where genius comes from. If we ran the world of painting the way we currently run the world of TV, Picasso would have gotten the vision for *Guernica*, and then he would have written a proposal to PPS (the Public Painting System). The title of the proposal would have been, "The *Guernica* Painting: A Proposal."

The *Guernica* Painting:
A Proposal for a Major Artwork

By Pablo Picasso

The Spanish Civil War is an event that has captured both the headlines of every major newspaper and the popular imagination of the nation. Yet what is the Spanish Civil War? What does it mean to the average person? I hope to capture this feeling through an intensive yet highly personal presentation of the impact of the fascist government's bombing of one small village: Guernica.

The work will be largely two-dimensional, painted on a canvass, with images of people, cows, and a lamp....

You get the idea.

Well, Picasso would write the proposal (along PPS published guidelines), and in time (say, about six months or so), the *Guernica* project would make its way through the PPS review system. It would be looked at, in committee, by a number of very well-known PPS painters, as well as administrators for the PPS system. They generally would like the proposal, and they even might fund it, but they would have some suggestions to make.

PPS
The Public Painting System

Dear Mr. Picasso,

Many thanks for your recent submission "The Guernica Painting Project." We at PPS read it with great interests, and I am delighted to tell you that you are on the "fast track" for approval for commencement of the painting.

We do, however, have a few small problems with the proposal, but we are sure that you will be amenable to making some changes to make the painting more "audience friendly."

1. *This is a war painting. As you know, it is not our practice to fund war paintings because they do not fall within the PPS guidelines for "good paintings." However, when we do fund war paintings, we have found that*

museum audiences generally respond best to some-thing heroic and a victory. (Washington Crossing the Delaware—both very heroic and uplifting—generated our greatest audience response during the museum fund-raising drive three years ago.) Your Guernica project, while dealing with a war, has neither a hero nor (how shall we put this?) a happy ending. Please rethink the focus of the painting. While the Spanish Civil War is a very noble and worthwhile subject with which to deal, we would rather see you focus one or two "heroic" personalities in the war (perhaps one Republican and one Fascist—to give an all-important sense of balance, something we really like around here).

2. *On another subject, we have spent a great deal of time (and money) on focus-grouping your most recent work. I have to tell you that audiences in our test markets of Cleveland and Parsippany, New Jersey, did not react particularly well to your work. This can, of course, be disappointing for an artist, but we have found that by paying attention to the results of focus grouping, we can greatly increase audience response numbers. When you come down to our offices in Washington, we will be happy to go over the specifics, but one point was driven home again and again: You must put the eyes back into the faces. People find this particularly distressing....*

This is, in fact, how TV is made. That, and once Picasso does get his funding for the *Guernica* Painting Project, he has to go out and "book" a union paintbrush holder, a union paint holder, and a union canvass mover. And, of course, all of them work only from 9 to 5, with an hour for lunch and a five-minute break every hour. They will, of course, work overtime, but that is at their discretion, and only for time and a half, which will drive up the budget for *Guernica*.

Well, of course, this is going to produce garbage. And this is what you see on TV. Garbage. And this is the reason that what you see on TV is garbage. Not because the people who work in it are dumb, but because the way we have "architected" the system is antithetical to creativity.

It's as though, with the invention of TV, we consciously set out to crush any way for the medium to foster creative vision.

If television were a marginal activity, like video art, we could afford to ignore it. To let it continue in its own meandering and painfully mediocre way. But television is not that. For better or for worst, it is the single most powerful medium of communication in the world today. And it would seem that it is only going to continue to grow in power and influence. And this is why it is critically important that we stop, at this juncture, and say, "Okay. We have been doing this all wrong up until now. But it is not too late. We must rethink how TV works, what it is, and how we use it."

Television did not arrive with an instruction manual when it was invented in 1939. It was just a technology, like any other. We decided what we would do with it and how we would use it.

Most of our decisions from 1939 to 1952 were based on what the technology of 1952 looked like. Cameras were huge, incredibly expensive, and difficult to use. Edit systems were the size of tractor trailers and cost a half-million dollars. They also were incredibly complex and difficult to use. The way that we decided to put people to work, the way that we elected to use the medium as a tool to produce product, was entirely a function of that 1952 heavy, complex, and expensive technology.

Today, all that technology is as obsolete as a tube-based Univac computer. But the way that we organize TV, and the way that we limit access, is still in place. It is as though we took those 1952 rules and cast them in stone for eternity.

And that decision, more than anything else, has served to destroy the great potential that television as a creative medium represents. We consciously do not allow anyone to be creative with the medium, preferring the safe, predictable path of repetition and banality.

But the new small digital technologies give us the opportunity to completely redefine how TV could work, who gets access to it, and how it is made.

Just as Picasso got an idea for a painting, went up to the studio, and started to paint, now someone with a vision for a TV project simply must pick up the camera, start to shoot, sit down at the computer, and start to edit. Maybe that person makes junk. Maybe he or she makes a *Guernica*.

So here's your chance. Take the camera or the iPhone, and go and make the content that is in your head and in your heart. Follow your instincts. Create and create and create again. And if you are talented and lucky, a fantastic future awaits you.

Index